Practical Bridge Endings

Chien-Hwa Wang

B. T. Batsford Ltd, *London*

First published 1997

© Chien-Hwa Wang

ISBN 0 7134 8143 9

A CIP catalogue record for this book is available from the British Library.

Typeset by Apsbridge Services Ltd, Nottingham.
Printed by Redwood Books, Trowbridge, Wiltshire
for the publishers,
B. T. Batsford Ltd,
583, Fulham Road,
London SW6 5BY

A BATSFORD BRIDGE BOOK
Series Editor: Tony Sowter

CONTENTS

INTRODUCTION

From thousands of recorded or reported bridge hands the author has selected the following sixty deals, which lead to various endings such as throw-in play, elimination play, simple squeeze, trump coup, double squeeze, outside trump play, triple squeeze, the Devil's Coup, repeated squeeze, smother play, ruffing squeeze, guard squeeze, optimal treatment of suit combinations, etc. It is hoped that the reader will find in this book something useful and interesting.

1
ELIMINATION

Love All. Dealer North.

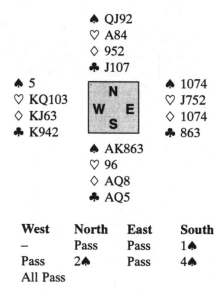

                    ♠ QJ92
                    ♡ A84
                    ◇ 952
                    ♣ J107

    ♠ 5   ♠ 1074
    ♡ KQ103   ♡ J752
    ◇ KJ63   ◇ 1074
    ♣ K942   ♣ 863

                    ♠ AK863
                    ♡ 96
                    ◇ AQ8
                    ♣ AQ5

West	North	East	South
–	Pass	Pass	1♠
Pass	2♠	Pass	4♠
All Pass			

Opening lead: ♡K

The declarer ducked West's opening lead of the king of hearts and West continued with the queen which dummy's ace won. Dummy's last heart was led and ruffed in the declarer's hand. The ace and jack of trumps won the next two tricks. Dummy led the jack of clubs on which East and South played low, and West followed with the two. Another club was led and South finessed the queen. But West won this trick with the king and returned the suit, hoping that by now East might be void of clubs. East, however, followed with a third club, and the declarer's ace won.

The declarer now led a spade to dummy's queen and the position was:

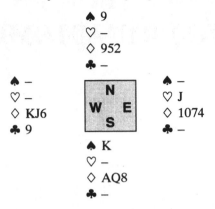

```
                    ♠ 9
                    ♡ –
                    ◇ 952
                    ♣ –
        ♠ –                      ♠ –
        ♡ –                      ♡ J
        ◇ KJ6                    ◇ 1074
        ♣ 9                      ♣ –
                    ♠ K
                    ♡ –
                    ◇ AQ8
                    ♣ –
```

The two of diamonds was led from dummy and South played the eight when East followed with the seven. West won with the jack, but he was obliged to lead a diamond into South's tenace or give the declarer a ruff and discard.

Note that the essential ingredient for an elimination and throw-in play to work is to remove any 'safe' exit cards from the victim's hand before 'throwing him in'. In this case, if declarer had played on diamonds before ruffing dummy's last heart, West would have been able to get off lead safely by returning a heart after winning the first diamond.

2
LET HIM RUN DIAMONDS

Game All. Dealer East.

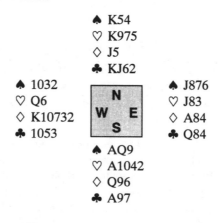

	♠ K54	
	♡ K975	
	◇ J5	
	♣ KJ62	
♠ 1032		♠ J876
♡ Q6		♡ J83
◇ K10732		◇ A84
♣ 1053		♣ Q84
	♠ AQ9	
	♡ A1042	
	◇ Q96	
	♣ A97	

West	North	East	South
–	–	Pass	1NT
Pass	2◇	Pass	2♡
Pass	3♡	Pass	3NT
All Pass			

Opening lead: ◇3

South bid a strong one no trump and North's two diamond bid was forcing Stayman. East won the first trick with the ace of diamonds and returned the eight of diamonds. West played the two and dummy's jack won. It was clear that West held originally five diamonds and East still had a diamond in his hand. It was also clear that, as soon as East or West gained the lead, they would immediately cash three diamond tricks to set the contract. To avoid defeat, the declarer should cross to the South hand with a spade, lead back the queen of diamonds, and let West take his three diamond winners.

Suppose West cashed all his three diamond winners, then dummy would discard a heart, a spade and a club in turn, and South would discard a club and a heart. North-South would regain the lead at Trick 7. After cashing some winners, the declarer would reach the following ending:

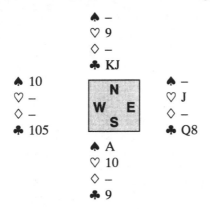

```
                    ♠ –
                    ♡ 9
                    ◇ –
                    ♣ KJ
      ♠ 10                        ♠ –
      ♡ –          ┌─────────┐    ♡ J
      ◇ –          │   N     │    ◇ –
      ♣ 105        │ W   E   │    ♣ Q8
                   │   S     │
                   └─────────┘
                    ♠ A
                    ♡ 10
                    ◇ –
                    ♣ 9
```

Now the ace of spades would be played, North discarding the nine of hearts, and East would be squeezed in hearts and clubs. In effect, if East discards the jack of hearts, South cashed the ten. Alternatively, if East throws a club, South can play a club to the king dropping East's queen.

If West won two diamond winners instead of three, then the declarer, on regaining the lead, would first concede a heart or a club to East, thus setting up the ninth trick for his contract.

Notice that when West ducked the second round of diamonds he was attempting to maintain communications for the defence. South thwarted this plan by cutting the defences communications and had the pleasure of watching West inflict a 'suicide squeeze' on his partner.

Also note that declarer still had to guess who had started with the queen of clubs. Of course, if East has to spend some time considering his discards then it will not be too difficult for declarer to guess the position.

3
WANG'S SQUEEZE

Love All. Dealer South.

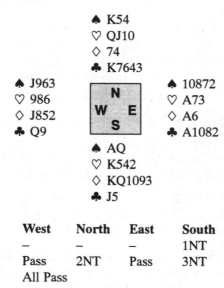

	♠ K54	
	♡ QJ10	
	◇ 74	
	♣ K7643	
♠ J963		♠ 10872
♡ 986		♡ A73
◇ J852		◇ A6
♣ Q9		♣ A1082
	♠ AQ	
	♡ K542	
	◇ KQ1093	
	♣ J5	

West	North	East	South
–	–	–	1NT
Pass	2NT	Pass	3NT
All Pass			

Opening lead: ♡9

I found this hand in my desk calendar. The date was 11 April 1993.

East won the first trick with the ace of hearts and returned a heart to dummy. The four of diamonds was led to the six, ten and jack. West led another heart. Dummy won and led the seven of diamonds to East's ace. East led a spade, South's ace winning. After three diamond winners were cashed, the position was:

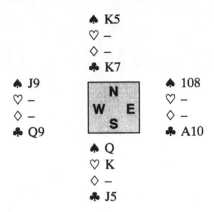

I led the king of hearts from my hand and both opponents were squeezed. West discarded the nine of clubs, dummy threw the seven and East discarded the eight of spades. The spade queen was cashed and the five of clubs was led to the queen, king and ace. My club jack won the last trick.

Had West thrown a spade instead of the nine of clubs at Trick 10, dummy would have made the same discard of the seven of clubs, and East would have had to discard the ten of clubs. The queen of spades Would have been cashed and a club led to East's ace. Dummy's king of spades would have won the last trick. Here is a similar position:

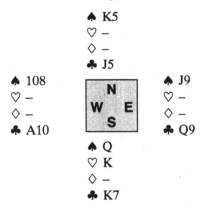

The lead of the king of hearts, on which dummy discards the five of clubs, squeezes West and East simultaneously. Whatever the opponents discard (they cannot both discard in spades), South just cashes the queen of spades and leads the seven of clubs. Either the king of spades or the king of clubs must win the last trick.

4
ESTABLISHING A TRICK

North-South Game. Dealer North.

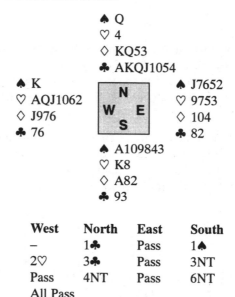

                    ♠ Q
                    ♡ 4
                    ◇ KQ53
                    ♣ AKQJ1054
    ♠ K   ♠ J7652
    ♡ AQJ1062   ♡ 9753
    ◇ J976   ◇ 104
    ♣ 76   ♣ 82
                    ♠ A109843
                    ♡ K8
                    ◇ A82
                    ♣ 93

West	North	East	South
–	1♣	Pass	1♠
2♡	3♣	Pass	3NT
Pass	4NT	Pass	6NT
All Pass			

Opening lead: ♣7

Playing a strong club system, one club showed 16+ points and one spade was a natural positive. When South bid 3NT, North raised speculatively and South was more than happy to bid the slam,

The declarer won the first trick with dummy's ten of clubs and led the queen of spades to South's ace, dropping West's king. A diamond was led to dummy's queen, and five rounds of clubs were played off. The position at Trick 9 was:

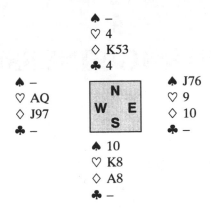

```
                ♠ —
                ♡ 4
                ◇ K53
                ♣ 4
 ♠ —                        ♠ J76
 ♡ AQ          N            ♡ 9
 ◇ J97      W     E         ◇ 10
 ♣ —           S            ♣ —
                ♠ 10
                ♡ K8
                ◇ A8
                ♣ —
```

Now the four of clubs was led from dummy, South discarded the ten of spades, and West was squeezed. If he discarded a diamond, North-South would win three diamond tricks. If he discarded the queen of hearts, dummy would lead the four of hearts. South would cover the nine with the king and the eight of hearts would win a trick.

Note that declarer is by no means certain to guess the ending right. For example, West could have started with the king and jack of spades and found the good play of the king of spades under the ace. Then, if South lets him take the ace of hearts, he would have the jack of spades to cash as well, and, just to add to South's chagrin, the diamonds would have been breaking 3-3 the whole time. In a similar way, West could have started with seven hearts including the nine which he had been careful to conceal all the way along, and once again South's play would fail.

In reality, with seven hearts, West might have bid more than two hearts and, especially in defence, most players are loath to part with a higher card than necessary. So, in all probability declarer would choose to play for the layout actually shown. However, you can't say that you haven't been warned.

5
AVOIDING FINESSES

East-West Game. Dealer South.

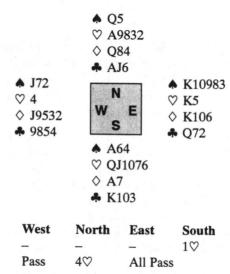

```
                    ♠ Q5
                    ♡ A9832
                    ◇ Q84
                    ♣ AJ6
    ♠ J72            ┌─────┐         ♠ K10983
    ♡ 4             │  N  │          ♡ K5
    ◇ J9532         │W   E│          ◇ K106
    ♣ 9854          │  S  │          ♣ Q72
                    └─────┘
                    ♠ A64
                    ♡ QJ1076
                    ◇ A7
                    ♣ K103
```

West	North	East	South
–	–	–	1♡
Pass	4♡	All Pass	

Opening lead: ♠2

West led the two of spades to the queen, king and ace. The declarer played the ace and seven of diamonds, and dummy's queen was lost to East's king. East cashed the ten of spades and exited with a diamond which South ruffed. The declarer took a finesse in hearts, but there was no luck. East won with the king and returned the suit. Finally, after drawing trumps the declarer took another finesse in clubs the wrong way, and, having lost one trick in each suit, that was one down.

Surely the declarer's play was rather poor. After the opening lead of the two of spades the contract is undefeatable provided the three outside trumps are not concentrated in one opponent's hand. The declarer should duck the first trick when East covers dummy's queen of spades with the king. East has no safe lead except a spade. The declarer wins with the ace of spades and ruffs a spade. The ace of diamonds is played, followed by the seven of diamonds. When East wins dummy's queen of diamonds with the king, his only harmless return is a diamond, which the declarer ruffs. Now the declarer plays the queen of hearts and puts on dummy's ace when West plays low. The king does not drop, and the position is as follows:

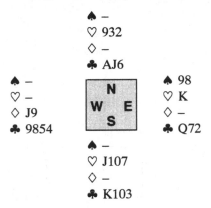

```
                 ♠ –
                 ♡ 932
                 ◇ –
                 ♣ AJ6
   ♠ –          ┌──────────┐    ♠ 98
   ♡ –          │    N     │    ♡ K
   ◇ J9         │  W     E │    ◇ –
   ♣ 9854       │    S     │    ♣ Q72
                └──────────┘
                 ♠ –
                 ♡ J107
                 ◇ –
                 ♣ K103
```

A trump is led from dummy. It does not matter which opponent holds the king of hearts. He wins the king and must give North-South the rest.

Suppose East wins in the position as shown. If he plays a spade, he gives declarer a 'ruff and discard'. Declarer can trump in either hand and throw away a losing cub from the other hand. Subsequently, declarer will be able to trump the third round of clubs. Alternatively, if East leads a club, declarer plays low from his own hand and will either score the jack in dummy, or be able to top the queen with the ace. Either way declarer's club loser disappears.

6
REDUCING
TWO LOSERS TO ONE

East-West Game. Dealer West.

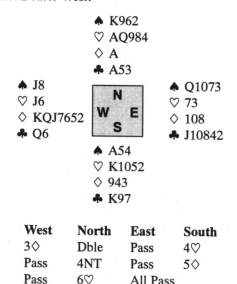

```
                    ♠ K962
                    ♡ AQ984
                    ◇ A
                    ♣ A53
    ♠ J8              N           ♠ Q1073
    ♡ J6          W     E         ♡ 73
    ◇ KQJ7652         S           ◇ 108
    ♣ Q6                          ♣ J10842
                    ♠ A54
                    ♡ K1052
                    ◇ 943
                    ♣ K97
```

West	North	East	South
3◇	Dble	Pass	4♡
Pass	4NT	Pass	5◇
Pass	6♡	All Pass	

Opening lead: ◇K

The declarer won the opening lead with dummy's ace of diamonds and cleared trumps in two rounds. A diamond was led from the South hand and ruffed in dummy, East following suit. The declarer cashed the ace-king of spades and the ace of clubs. West followed with the eight and jack of spades and the six of clubs. Now, the declarer had to make the right choice.

Since West had opened three diamonds, it was a fair bet that he had seven diamonds. If West's cards were 3-2-7-1, the declarer should concede a spade trick and set up dummy's fourth spade as a winner. But, if West's cards were 2-2-7-2, the declarer has to cash the king of clubs. The position would be as follows:

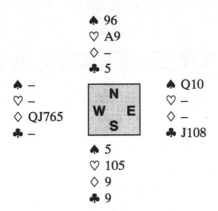

The nine of diamonds is led, West has to cover with an honour (otherwise the club would be discarded from dummy), and dummy discards the five of clubs. West now has no choice but to lead another diamond. Dummy ruffs while South discards a spade. By conceding a diamond trick to West, declarer has reduced two losers to one.

7
EARLY ENDPLAY

Game All. Dealer North.

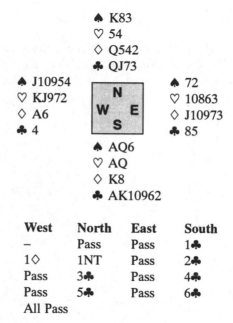

```
                        ♠ K83
                        ♡ 54
                        ◇ Q542
                        ♣ QJ73
        ♠ J10954                        ♠ 72
        ♡ KJ972          N              ♡ 10863
        ◇ A6         W       E          ◇ J10973
        ♣ 4             S              ♣ 85
                        ♠ AQ6
                        ♡ AQ
                        ◇ K8
                        ♣ AK10962
```

West	North	East	South
–	Pass	Pass	1♣
1◇	1NT	Pass	2♣
Pass	3♣	Pass	4♣
Pass	5♣	Pass	6♣
All Pass			

Opening lead: ♠J

After South's strong club opening, West's one diamond bid was conventional, it showed both majors. East was too weak to compete.

The opening lead was won with South's ace and trumps were drawn in two rounds, West discarding a heart on the second round. The king and queen of spades were cashed. East discarded a diamond on the queen of spades. The declarer now knew that West held originally five spades and one trump. From West's bidding, declarer also suspected that he held the ace of diamonds and, since he had a heart suit as well, his diamonds were likely to be a short suit, probably a singleton or doubleton. Consequently, it was not that difficult to make the contract. The position at Trick 6 was:

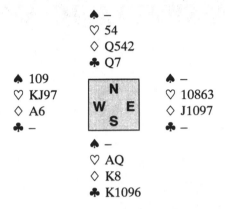

♠ —
♡ 54
◊ Q542
♣ Q7

♠ 109
♡ KJ97
◊ A6
♣ —

♠ —
♡ 10863
◊ J1097
♣ —

♠ —
♡ AQ
◊ K8
♣ K1096

Now the eight of diamonds was led. If West played the ace, South's queen of hearts could be discarded on dummy's queen of diamonds. If West followed with the six, dummy's queen would win, and West would be thrown in by the lead of a diamond at the next trick.

That would leave West with the unenviable prospect of either returning a spade, conceding a ruff and discard, or leading a heart away from his king around to declarer's tenace.

8
A SIMPLE PLAY

North-South Game. Dealer East.

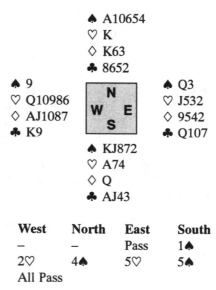

♠ A10654
♡ K
◇ K63
♣ 8652

♠ 9
♡ Q10986
◇ AJ1087
♣ K9

♠ Q3
♡ J532
◇ 9542
♣ Q107

♠ KJ872
♡ A74
◇ Q
♣ AJ43

West	North	East	South
–	–	Pass	1♠
2♡	4♠	5♡	5♠
All Pass			

Opening lead: ♡10

Dummy's singleton king of hearts won the first trick and a diamond was led to the two, queen and ace. West returned the jack of diamonds, dummy played low and South ruffed. The declarer played the ace-king of spades, followed by the ace of clubs and ace of hearts, on which a club was discarded from dummy. Now a heart was led and ruffed. Dummy cashed the king of diamonds, South discarding a club, and the position was:

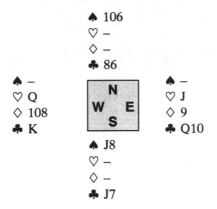

♠ 106
♡ –
◇ –
♣ 86

♠ –
♡ Q
◇ 108
♣ K

♠ –
♡ J
◇ 9
♣ Q10

♠ J8
♡ –
◇ –
♣ J7

The declarer led a club from North. Although the K, Q, 10, 9 and 7 were in the opponents' hands originally, the declarer lost only one trick in clubs. West had to return a heart or a diamond to give North-South a ruff and discard.

In this hand the declarer's work was quite simple. He simply cashed the top winners in each suit and ruffed two small cards. It is easy to see that the declarer handled the club suit successfully. This play would succeed if the opponents' clubs split three-two and the king and the queen were divided in the two hands. It would fail only if either opponent held king-queen-small, or if West held king-ten-small or queen-ten-small while East unblocked the queen or the king on the lead of the ace of clubs.

9

HE RUFFED MY ACE

North-South Game. Dealer West.

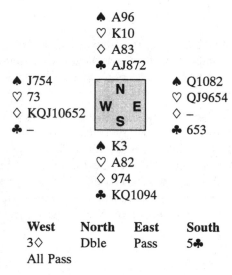

	♠ A96	
	♡ K10	
	◇ A83	
	♣ AJ872	

♠ J754		♠ Q1082
♡ 73		♡ QJ9654
◇ KQJ10652		◇ –
♣ –		♣ 653

	♠ K3	
	♡ A82	
	◇ 974	
	♣ KQ1094	

West	North	East	South
3◇	Dble	Pass	5♣
All Pass			

Opening lead: ◇K

North's initial double was optional, and with no diamond stopper South opted for the obvious game contract. It is worth noting that North's alternative (and superior) bid of 3NT would have been an easier contract.

Dummy's ace of diamonds was ruffed by East, who returned the queen of hearts to dummy's king. The declarer believed that East probably had the jack and nine of hearts because he had returned the queen. After drawing trumps the declarer played three rounds of spades, South ruffing the third round. Dummy was entered with a trump and the ten of hearts was led.

East covered with the jack and South's ace won. The eight of hearts was now led. When West discarded a diamond, dummy, instead of ruffing, also discarded a diamond. East had to win with the nine of hearts. The position was:

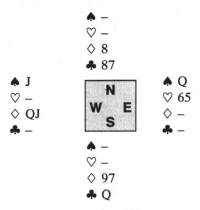

```
              ♠ —
              ♡ —
              ◇ 8
              ♣ 87
♠ J                        ♠ Q
♡ —        ┌───────┐       ♡ 65
◇ QJ       │   N   │       ◇ —
♣ —        │ W   E │       ♣ —
           │   S   │
           └───────┘
              ♠ —
              ♡ —
              ◇ 97
              ♣ Q
```

East had to lead a spade or a heart. This gave the declarer a ruff and discard to make the contract.

10
TRUMP REDUCING

East-West Game. Dealer North.

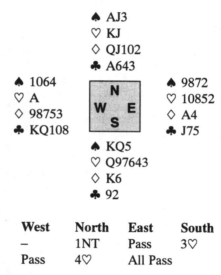

	♠ AJ3	
	♡ KJ	
	◇ QJ102	
	♣ A643	

♠ 1064		♠ 9872
♡ A		♡ 10852
◇ 98753		◇ A4
♣ KQ108		♣ J75

	♠ KQ5	
	♡ Q97643	
	◇ K6	
	♣ 92	

West	North	East	South
–	1NT	Pass	3♡
Pass	4♡	All Pass	

Opening lead: ♣K

Dummy won the opening lead and led the king of hearts to West's ace. West led two more rounds of clubs, South ruffing the second. The declarer led a small trump to dummy's jack, West discarding the three of diamonds. There remained in the East hand the ten and the eight of trumps, while the declarer had the queen and the nine. But dummy was now void of trumps, so it was impossible to take a finesse against East's ten.

At Trick 6, a small diamond was led to South's king. The six of diamonds was led to dummy's ten and East's ace. East returned a spade, which was taken by dummy's jack. The declarer now played the queen of diamonds, but East refused to ruff. South, instead of discarding a spade, ruffed with a small trump, thus reducing his trumps to the same length as East's. South

led the queen of spades to dummy's ace, leaving the following three card
end position:

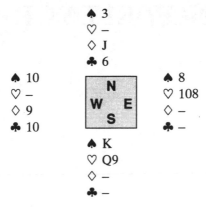

```
                    ♠ 3
                    ♡ –
                    ◊ J
                    ♣ 6
   ♠ 10         ┌─────────┐         ♠ 8
   ♡ –          │    N    │         ♡ 108
   ◊ 9          │ W     E │         ◊ –
   ♣ 10         │    S    │         ♣ –
                └─────────┘
                    ♠ K
                    ♡ Q9
                    ◊ –
                    ♣ –
```

Dummy led the jack of diamonds. North-South won the remaining three
tricks regardless of East's defence. If East ruffed, South would overruff,
and the king of spades would win the last trick. If East discarded the eight
of spades, South would also discard his spade. Whatever card North led to
the penultimate trick, East would be forced to ruff. South would overruff,
killing East's two trumps in turn.

11
NO DEFENCE

East-West Game. Dealer North.

♠ 872
♡ J9872
◇ A7
♣ 1064

```
    N
  W   E
    S
```

♠ AJ3
♡ AKQ543
◇ 8
♣ AJ5

West	North	East	South
–	Pass	Pass	4♡
All Pass			

Opening lead: ◇K

After dummy's ace of diamonds won the first trick, how should South play?

The declarer's problem is to limit his losers in spades and clubs to three tricks. He should plan his play this way: He leads the seven of diamonds at Trick 2 and ruffs it with the queen of hearts. The ace, king, jack, and nine of hearts are played, reducing the position to:

♠ 872
♡ 8
◇ –
♣ 1064

♠ AJ3
♡ 5
◇ –
♣ AJ5

A spade is now led from dummy.

If East follows with a small spade, South plays the jack, and West wins. Now, if West returns a club, the declarer can set up a club winner. So West has to lead a spade. South wins with the ace and leads back another spade. Whether West or East wins this trick, he must lead a club, which will help the declarer to set up a club winner; or he may lead any other card to give the declarer a ruff and discard.

On the first round of spades, if East plays the king or the queen, the declarer ducks. East may lead a spade, then South wins with the ace and leads back the jack of spades, and the result is the same as above. If East leads a small club, South follows with the five. If West wins this trick, he is thrown in. The declarer now has the ace-jack of spades and ace-jack of clubs in his hand.

12
AGAINST GOSPEL

North-South Game. Dealer North.

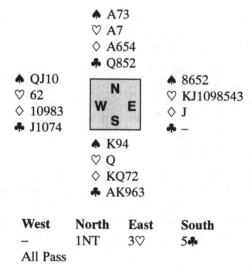

	♠ A73	
	♡ A7	
	◇ A654	
	♣ Q852	
♠ QJ10		♠ 8652
♡ 62		♡ KJ1098543
◇ 10983		◇ J
♣ J1074		♣ —
	♠ K94	
	♡ Q	
	◇ KQ72	
	♣ AK963	

West	North	East	South
–	1NT	3♡	5♣
	All Pass		

Opening lead: ♠Q

The declarer won the opening lead with the king of spades and led a small trump to dummy's queen, East discarding a heart. North-South lost one trick each in spades, diamonds and clubs, so the contract was one down.

The declarer explained that he cashed the queen of clubs first to protect against East's holding all four trumps, in which case North-South would be able to avoid losing a trump trick.

This is indeed a safety play. But it is not a sound analysis for this hand. East had bid three hearts. It was West, not East, who was more likely to hold all four trumps.

In fact, the correct play is to lay down the ace of clubs at Trick 2. On seeing East's discard of a heart, the declarer can cash three top diamonds, the ace of spades, the ace of hearts, and ruff a heart to reach this ending:

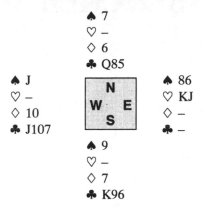

```
              ♠ 7
              ♡ –
              ◇ 6
              ♣ Q85
 ♠ J        ┌─────────┐      ♠ 86
 ♡ –        │    N    │      ♡ KJ
 ◇ 10       │  W   E  │      ◇ –
 ♣ J107     │    S    │      ♣ –
            └─────────┘
              ♠ 9
              ♡ –
              ◇ 7
              ♣ K96
```

The declarer now leads a spade or a diamond to throw West in. West can take his two winners in spades and diamonds, but he has to concede all three trump tricks to North-South.

If he leads a small card, South will win cheaply and take the last two tricks with the two top trumps. If he leads the jack or the ten, South wins with his king and takes the marked finesse through the West hand.

13
BLOCKED

East-West Game. Dealer West.

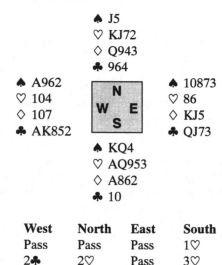

	♠ J5	
	♡ KJ72	
	◇ Q943	
	♣ 964	
♠ A962		♠ 10873
♡ 104		♡ 86
◇ 107		◇ KJ5
♣ AK852		♣ QJ73
	♠ KQ4	
	♡ AQ953	
	◇ A862	
	♣ 10	

West	North	East	South
Pass	Pass	Pass	1♡
2♣	2♡	Pass	3♡
Pass	4♡	All Pass	

Opening lead: ♣K

West won the first trick with the king of clubs and continued with the ace, which South ruffed.

The declarer played spades before clearing the trumps, and found that the ace of spades was in the West hand. He was sure that West did not also hold the king of diamonds as otherwise West would have made an opening bid.

The declarer discarded a diamond from dummy on South's spade winner, led a trump to dummy, and led and ruffed dummy's last club. He played another trump to dummy, discovering that the outside trumps were evenly divided. Prospects had improved and there was now some hope of making the contract, the situation being:

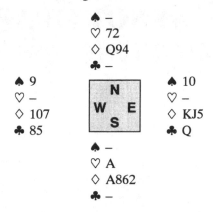

♠ —
♡ 72
◇ Q94
♣ —

♠ 9
♡ —
◇ 107
♣ 85

♠ 10
♡ —
◇ KJ5
♣ Q

♠ —
♡ A
◇ A862
♣ —

Dummy led the queen of diamonds, and East had to cover with the king. South won with the ace and led a small diamond. The contract was thus made, because the jack and ten of diamonds were divided in the East-West hands. If West holds the lead with the ten he is endplayed to to concede a ruff and discard, and East cannot overtake without establishing the diamonds for declarer.

This was not a very difficult hand, but the order of the cards played was important. In particular, it was important that declarer didn't prematurely waste his entries to the dummy. One entry was needed to ruff a club and the other to lead the queen of diamonds off the dummy.

14
HE CANNOT GUARD BOTH SUITS

North-South Game. Dealer West.

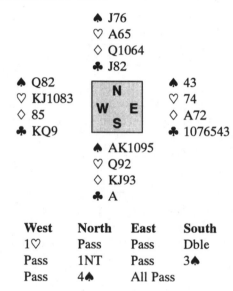

```
                      ♠ J76
                      ♡ A65
                      ◇ Q1064
                      ♣ J82
        ♠ Q82                        ♠ 43
        ♡ KJ1083        N            ♡ 74
        ◇ 85         W     E         ◇ A72
        ♣ KQ9           S            ♣ 1076543
                      ♠ AK1095
                      ♡ Q92
                      ◇ KJ93
                      ♣ A
```

West	North	East	South
1♡	Pass	Pass	Dble
Pass	1NT	Pass	3♠
Pass	4♠	All Pass	

Opening lead: ◇8

The eight of diamonds was led to the four, seven and jack. Expecting West to have the queen of spades, declarer played the ace and king of trumps, and, when the queen did not drop, he followed with the nine of diamonds to East's ace. East returned the seven of hearts to South's nine and West's ten. Knowing that West had the king of hearts it was routine for declarer to play dummy's five as West could not continue the suit safely.

After cashing the queen of spades, West led the king of clubs to South's
ace. The declarer cashed the queen and king of diamonds and played a
trump winner. The position was:

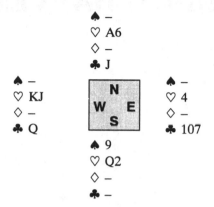

The declarer led the nine of spades and West had to make a discard before
North. If he discarded the jack of hearts, the ace and queen of hearts would
win two tricks. If he discarded the queen of clubs, dummy's ace of hearts
and jack of clubs would win the last two tricks.

West was forced to discard a winner or a guard to a potential winner
because he lacked room for retaining both. Had East held West's cards, the
squeeze would not have worked.

15
RANDOM HARVEST

Game All. Dealer North.

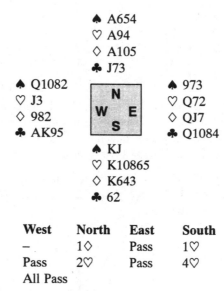

```
                    ♠ A654
                    ♡ A94
                    ◇ A105
                    ♣ J73
  ♠ Q1082                        ♠ 973
  ♡ J3              N             ♡ Q72
  ◇ 982         W       E         ◇ QJ7
  ♣ AK95            S             ♣ Q1084
                    ♠ KJ
                    ♡ K10865
                    ◇ K643
                    ♣ 62
```

West	North	East	South
–	1◇	Pass	1♡
Pass	2♡	Pass	4♡
All Pass			

Opening lead: ♣K

North-South were playing Precision, so North's one diamond opener didn't guarantee the suit. South's raise to game was a little ambitious. He was fortunate to find fairly suitable cards in the dummy.

The declarer had a trump loser and a diamond loser. The contract would be defeated unless one of the opponents held queen-jack doubleton in hearts or diamonds. Accordingly, the declarer played the ace-king of trumps and the ace-king of diamonds. But there was no luck and the contract was one down.

Was there any way to make the contract? Yes. The declarer should first cash two top diamond and two top spade winners. A spade would then be led from dummy and ruffed in the declarer's hand. Now the declarer would lead a third round of diamonds, allowing East's queen to win. The position would be:

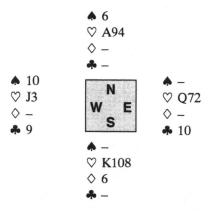

```
              ♠ 6
              ♡ A94
              ◇ -
              ♣ -
  ♠ 10                      ♠ -
  ♡ J3        ┌────────┐    ♡ Q72
  ◇ -         │   N    │    ◇ -
  ♣ 9         │ W    E │    ♣ 10
              │   S    │
              └────────┘
              ♠ -
              ♡ K108
              ◇ 6
              ♣ -
```

If East leads a trump, North-South would win three trump tricks together with a diamond winner. Alternatively, if East leads the ten of clubs, South would discard the six of diamonds, and dummy would ruff. Dummy then would lead the six of spades. If East ruffed low, South would over-ruff with the eight and win the three remaining trump tricks; if East ruffed with the queen, South would overruff with the king and take a finesse against West's jack at the next trick.

While this is another good example of elimination play, it is worth noting that declarer does not ruff out all his side losers. The play only succeeds because it was West who had the remaining spade, not East. A good example of 'partial elimination'.

16
ONE SUIT THROW-IN

Game All. Dealer West.

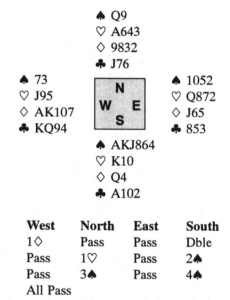

```
              ♠ Q9
              ♡ A643
              ◇ 9832
              ♣ J76
♠ 73                        ♠ 1052
♡ J95          N            ♡ Q872
◇ AK107      W   E          ◇ J65
♣ KQ94         S            ♣ 853
              ♠ AKJ864
              ♡ K10
              ◇ Q4
              ♣ A102
```

West	North	East	South
1◇	Pass	Pass	Dble
Pass	1♡	Pass	2♠
Pass	3♠	Pass	4♠
All Pass			

Opening lead: ◇K

West led three rounds of diamonds, South ruffing the third round. Trumps were cleared in three rounds. The declarer thought that West probably held the king-queen of clubs to justify his opening bid. He cashed the king of hearts and arrived at this position:

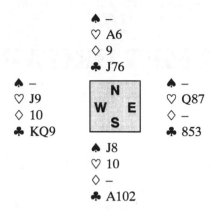

The jack of spades was led and West,who could not throw away a club without allowing declarer to establish the clubs easily, had to discard a heart or a diamond. If West discarded a heart, the declarer could lead the ten of hearts to dummy's ace, ruff a diamond, and lead the two of clubs to throw West in. The declarer's purpose was to eliminate from the West hand all cards apart from the clubs.

Even if East had a diamond higher than dummy's nine, and West discarded the ten of diamonds on the lead of the jack of spades, the declarer could still cash the ace of hearts, ruff a heart, and then lead a low club to endplay West.

17
TRUMP THROW-IN

Love All. Dealer North.

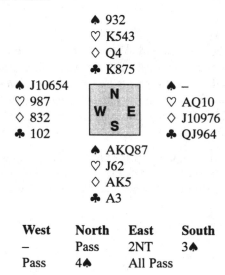

	♠ 932	
	♡ K543	
	◇ Q4	
	♣ K875	
♠ J10654		♠ –
♡ 987		♡ AQ10
◇ 832		◇ J10976
♣ 102		♣ QJ964
	♠ AKQ87	
	♡ J62	
	◇ AK5	
	♣ A3	

West	North	East	South
–	Pass	2NT	3♠
Pass	4♠	All Pass	

Opening lead: ♡9

East's two no trumps was an artificial bid, showing both minor suits, usually of five cards or longer. East won the first two heart tricks and played a third heart, South's jack winning. The declarer played the ace of spades, getting the bad news when East discarded a club.

After cashing the three diamond winners and two club winners, the declarer played the king of spades to arrive at the following ending:

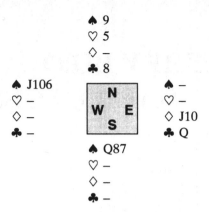

Now the seven of spades was led, and West was thrown in. He had to lead into the declarer's major tenace in the trump suit. His opponent's two natural trump tricks had been converted to only one.

18
THEY BOTH
UNGUARD CLUBS

East-West Game. Dealer West.

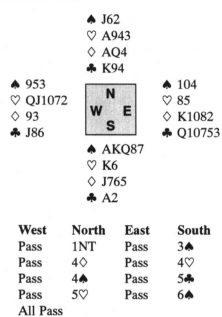

                    ♠ J62
                    ♡ A943
                    ◇ AQ4
                    ♣ K94

    ♠ 953   ♠ 104
    ♡ QJ1072   ♡ 85
    ◇ 93   ◇ K1082
    ♣ J86   ♣ Q10753

                    ♠ AKQ87
                    ♡ K6
                    ◇ J765
                    ♣ A2

West	North	East	South
Pass	1NT	Pass	3♠
Pass	4◇	Pass	4♡
Pass	4♠	Pass	5♣
Pass	5♡	Pass	6♠
All Pass			

Opening lead: ♡Q

After South's natural jump in spades, North showed his maximum by cuebidding on the way to four spades. When two cuebids from South drew a further cuebid out of North, South was able to bid the fair slam.

The declarer's king of hearts won the first trick. Trumps were drawn in three rounds. A diamond was led to dummy's queen and East's king. East returned a heart to West's ten and dummy's ace. Dummy led a heart, East discarded a club, and South ruffed. The ace and jack of diamonds were cashed, West discarding a heart on the jack of diamonds. The declarer now knew that West had the jack of hearts and East had the ten of diamonds left. The position was:

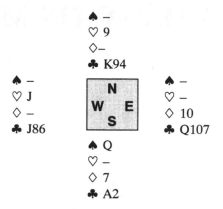

```
                    ♠ –
                    ♡ 9
                    ◇ –
                    ♣ K94
      ♠ –           ┌─────────┐         ♠ –
      ♡ J           │    N    │         ♡ –
      ◇ –           │ W     E │         ◇ 10
      ♣ J86         │    S    │         ♣ Q107
                    └─────────┘
                    ♠ Q
                    ♡ –
                    ◇ 7
                    ♣ A2
```

The declarer played the queen of spades and both opponents were squeezed. West had to discard a club, whereupon dummy's nine of hearts was discarded. East, knowing that the declarer had a diamond in his hand, also had to discard a club. The declarer won the last three tricks with the ace, king and nine of clubs.

A classical 'double squeeze' but note its positional nature. If East had the long hearts and West the long diamonds, the squeeze would not have operated, as dummy has to discard before East.

19
TOO MANY TRUMPS

East-West Game. Dealer East.

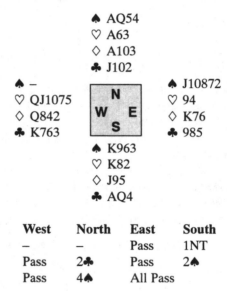

```
              ♠ AQ54
              ♡ A63
              ◊ A103
              ♣ J102
♠ —                          ♠ J10872
♡ QJ1075      N              ♡ 94
◊ Q842      W   E            ◊ K76
♣ K763        S              ♣ 985
              ♠ K963
              ♡ K82
              ◊ J95
              ♣ AQ4
```

West	North	East	South
–	–	Pass	1NT
Pass	2♣	Pass	2♠
Pass	4♠	All Pass	

Opening lead: ♡Q

South arrived in the normal contract of four spades after North had used Stayman to look for a 4-4 fit. The declarer won the first trick with dummy's ace of hearts and played the ace of spades, disclosing that all five trumps to the jack-ten were concentrated in the East hand.

The jack of clubs was led, East and South played low, and West won with the king. West led the jack of hearts to South's king. The five of diamonds was led to the two, ten and king. East returned a club to South's ace. The declarer led another diamond and finessed again, and this time the finesse succeeded. After cashing the diamond and club winners the declarer faced the following ending:

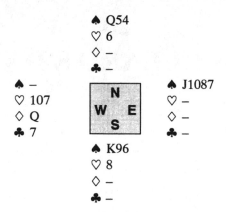

♠ Q54
♡ 6
◊ –
♣ –

♠ –
♡ 107
◊ Q
♣ 7

♠ J1087
♡ –
◊ –
♣ –

♠ K96
♡ 8
◊ –
♣ –

The declarer exited with a heart, and East was forced to ruff. Any return by East would give South the rest. The unhappy East had got too many trumps in his hand.

20
AS CLEAR AS DAY

Game All. Dealer East.

♠ KQ5
♡ AQ6
◇ KQ983
♣ KQ

♠ A974
♡ KJ4
◇ A102
♣ AJ9

West	North	East	South
–	–	Pass	1NT
Pass	2♣	Pass	2♠
Pass	4NT	Pass	5♠
Pass	5NT	Pass	6◇
Pass	7NT	All Pass	

Opening lead: ♡10

North-South have twelve top winners. If the diamonds break three-two or the spades break three-three, the contract is safe.

But the declarer must prepare for the worst. In order to keep the two-way finesse situation in diamonds, the declarer can cash only one diamond winner in dummy, and dummy must retain two entries besides the diamond suit. The declarer should play top winners in other suits, which will help explore the opponents' hand patterns.

So, the declarer won the first trick with his jack of hearts and led a diamond to dummy's queen, both opponents following suit. The declarer played three rounds of clubs. Dummy discarded a diamond and East a heart. Three rounds of spades were cashed, and on the third round East discarded another heart. Now the declarer knew that West held originally six clubs and four spades to the jack. Since he had shown a heart and a diamond, he had originally at most two diamonds. The declarer then played the four of hearts to dummy's queen, both opponents followed suit. All the cards were now as clear as day. West's hand pattern was 4-2-1-6. The situation had became:

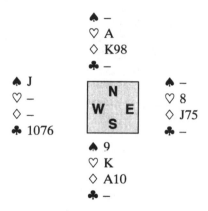

```
                 ♠ –
                 ♡ A
                 ◊ K98
                 ♣ –
  ♠ J          ┌─────────┐        ♠ –
  ♡ –          │    N    │        ♡ 8
  ◊ –          │  W   E  │        ◊ J75
  ♣ 1076       │    S    │        ♣ –
               └─────────┘
                 ♠ 9
                 ♡ K
                 ◊ A10
                 ♣ –
```

Dummy led a small diamond. South finessed the ten. After the ace of diamonds was cashed, dummy still had the carefully preserved heart entry to cash the king of diamonds.

Notice the importance of retaining your options as long as possible. Without this specific distribution, declarer would have cashed the ace of hearts and hoped that the diamonds were breaking or that one opponent had started with four diamonds and four spades – in which case he would have already been squeezed.

21
TWO RUFFING MENACES

Love All. Dealer North.

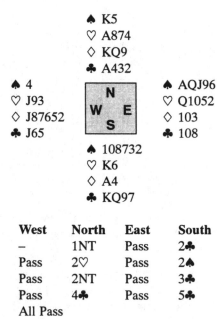

	♠ K5	
	♡ A874	
	◇ KQ9	
	♣ A432	

♠ 4		♠ AQJ96
♡ J93		♡ Q1052
◇ J87652		◇ 103
♣ J65		♣ 108

	♠ 108732	
	♡ K6	
	◇ A4	
	♣ KQ97	

West	North	East	South
–	1NT	Pass	2♣
Pass	2♡	Pass	2♠
Pass	2NT	Pass	3♣
Pass	4♣	Pass	5♣
All Pass			

Opening lead: ♠4

With top cards in both red suits and such poor spades, South would have done better to raise 2NT to 3NT. As it was South bid out the shape of his hand and so had the problem of how to make 11 tricks in clubs. Still, the play is the thing.

East won the first trick with the jack of spades and returned a trump, which South's king won. Another spade was led, West discarded a diamond, and dummy's king went to East's ace. East returned another trump to South's queen. The declarer cleared the outside trumps by leading a club to dummy's ace. After the ace and queen of diamonds were cashed the position was:

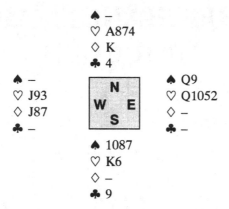

```
                    ♠ −
                    ♡ A874
                    ◊ K
                    ♣ 4
     ♠ −                              ♠ Q9
     ♡ J93            N               ♡ Q1052
     ◊ J87        W       E           ◊ −
     ♣ −              S               ♣ −
                    ♠ 1087
                    ♡ K6
                    ◊ −
                    ♣ 9
```

Now the king of diamonds was led from dummy, South discarding a spade, and East was ruffing-squeezed in spades and hearts. If East discarded a spade, the declarer could ruff out the queen of spades establishing a spade winner. If East discarded a heart, the declarer could cash the king and ace of hearts and ruff out a heart winner.

This was an automatic ruffing squeeze. West would have been squeezed if he had held East's cards.

22
THE CHANCES ARE DOUBLED

Love All. Dealer North.

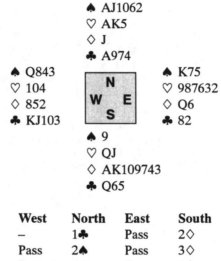

```
                    ♠ AJ1062
                    ♡ AK5
                    ◇ J
                    ♣ A974
      ♠ Q843          N          ♠ K75
      ♡ 104                      ♡ 987632
      ◇ 852       W     E        ◇ Q6
      ♣ KJ103         S          ♣ 82
                    ♠ 9
                    ♡ QJ
                    ◇ AK109743
                    ♣ Q65
```

West	North	East	South
–	1♣	Pass	2◇
Pass	2♠	Pass	3◇
Pass	4♣	Pass	4◇
Pass	4NT	Pass	5◇
Pass	5NT	Pass	7◇
All Pass			

Opening lead: ♡10

This hand was sent to me by Mr Shi Yunsheng. He was playing a strong club system and arrived in the poor grand slam after the injudicious use of Blackwood and the Grand Slam Force by his partner.

As South he won the opening lead with the jack of hearts and played the ace and king of trumps, dropping East's queen. After clearing the trumps he ruffed two spades and made the grand slam through a positional simple squeeze against West in spades and clubs.

This play succeeds if West has either the king-queen of spades or not less than four spades as well as the king of clubs.

A different play can greatly increase the chances of success. Either opponent will be subjected to a ruffing squeeze if he holds the king of clubs and four or more spades. The declarer draws trumps, ruffs a spade, and plays on trumps. At Trick 9, with the original East-West cards transposed, the position will be as follows:

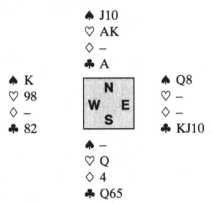

```
                    ♠ J10
                    ♡ AK
                    ◇ –
                    ♣ A
        ♠ K        ┌─────────┐      ♠ Q8
        ♡ 98       │    N    │      ♡ –
        ◇ –        │  W   E  │      ◇ –
        ♣ 82       │    S    │      ♣ KJ10
                   └─────────┘
                    ♠ –
                    ♡ Q
                    ◇ 4
                    ♣ Q65
```

The queen of hearts is led to dummy's king. West and East have no difficulty in discarding. At the next trick the ace of hearts is played, and the opponent who has still kept the king-small of clubs and king-small (or queen-small) of spades is squeezed. If he discards a spade, dummy's jack of spades can be ruffed out; if he discards a club, dummy's ace of clubs drops the king and South's queen becomes a winner.

23
ENTRYLESS TENACE

East-West Game. Dealer West.

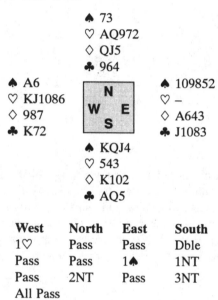

	♠ 73	
	♡ AQ972	
	◇ QJ5	
	♣ 964	
♠ A6		♠ 109852
♡ KJ1086		♡ –
◇ 987		◇ A643
♣ K72		♣ J1083
	♠ KQJ4	
	♡ 543	
	◇ K102	
	♣ AQ5	

West	North	East	South
1♡	Pass	Pass	Dble
Pass	Pass	1♠	1NT
Pass	2NT	Pass	3NT
All Pass			

Opening lead: ♡J

The declarer let West win the first trick with the jack of hearts, and West switched to the nine of diamonds, and East took dummy's queen with the ace. East returned the jack of clubs, on which South played the ace. The king of spades was led. West won with the ace and exited with a diamond which South won in hand. The declarer led a heart to West's six and dummy's seven. After cashing a diamond winner and a spade winner the situation was:

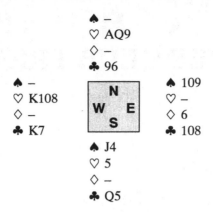

```
              ♠ −
              ♡ AQ9
              ◊ −
              ♣ 96
♠ −                        ♠ 109
♡ K108      ┌───────┐      ♡ −
◊ −         │   N   │      ◊ 6
♣ K7        │ W   E │      ♣ 108
            │   S   │
            └───────┘
              ♠ J4
              ♡ 5
              ◊ −
              ♣ Q5
```

The jack of spades was now played. If West discarded a heart, dummy could win three heart tricks. West actually discarded the seven of clubs, so declarer pitched a club from dummy and led a heart to the eight and nine before exiting with a club. West won and had to lead a heart into dummy's tenace.

Notice that, when West discarded a club, declarer could also have made the contract by throwing a heart from the dummy and setting up a club trick.

24
THREE CLUB TRICKS

North-South Game. Dealer East.

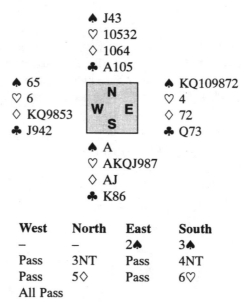

♠ J43
♡ 10532
◇ 1064
♣ A105

♠ 65
♡ 6
◇ KQ9853
♣ J942

♠ KQ109872
♡ 4
◇ 72
♣ Q73

♠ A
♡ AKQJ987
◇ AJ
♣ K86

West	North	East	South
–	–	2♠	3♠
Pass	3NT	Pass	4NT
Pass	5◇	Pass	6♡
All Pass			

Opening lead: ♠6

South's three spade bid showed a game-going hand. On the next round, he asked for aces and then, riding his luck, he bludgeoned his way to the heart slam.

The declarer won the first trick with the ace of spades and played the ace-king-queen-ten of trumps. Dummy led a small diamond to South's jack and West's king. West returned the five of spades, the declarer ruffed and played the ace of diamonds and another heart. The position was:

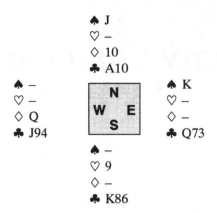

Now the nine of hearts was played. West could not discard the queen of diamonds, so he had to discard a club. North discarded the ten of diamonds. East could not discard the king of spades, so he also had to discard a club. Thus, the declarer collected three club tricks to make the six heart contract.

Another good example of a double squeeze with positional threats against both defenders. Notice that declarer could not really go wrong as he knew that East had the king of spades, therefore he had to keep the jack of spades in the dummy. If West had had all the clubs and East the queen of diamonds, the slam would have gone down but then there would have been no way to make it.

25
WHY YOU LOSE
AT BRIDGE

North-South Game. Dealer North.

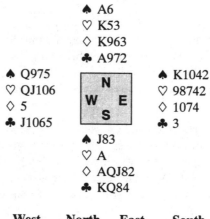

	♠ A6	
	♡ K53	
	◇ K963	
	♣ A972	
♠ Q975		♠ K1042
♡ QJ106		♡ 98742
◇ 5		◇ 1074
♣ J1065		♣ 3
	♠ J83	
	♡ A	
	◇ AQJ82	
	♣ KQ84	

West	North	East	South
–	1NT	Pass	2◇
Pass	2NT	Pass	3◇
Pass	4◇	Pass	4NT
Pass	5♠	Pass	6◇
All Pass			

Opening lead: ♡Q

South's two diamond bid was game forcing Stayman and North's five spade response showed two aces and the king of diamonds.

The declarer won the opening lead with the ace of hearts. After drawing trumps he played the ace and king of clubs, East discarding a heart on the king of clubs. With an inescapable loser in each black suit, the contract was one down.

It's a pity that an unbeatable contract was defeated. The declarer should draw three rounds of trumps, discard a spade from the closed hand on dummy's king of hearts, ruff dummy's last heart with a trump, and play the ace of spades and king (or queen) of clubs to arrive at this position:

♠ 6
♡ –
◇ 9
♣ A97

♠ J
♡ –
◇ J
♣ Q84

The jack of spades would now be led. Either of the opponents might win this trick, which would be their last trick. If the clubs divided three and two, there would be no problem. If the clubs were four-one or five-zero, the opponent's lead would give North-South three club tricks or a ruff and discard.

Notice that once declarer had discovered the actual distribution it was too late to do anything about it. This is a frequent problem which the expert will address by thinking he is in an excellent and seemingly easy contract. It is then that the good dummy player will ask the question 'What can go wrong?'

26
UNDERRUFFING

East-West Game. Dealer West.

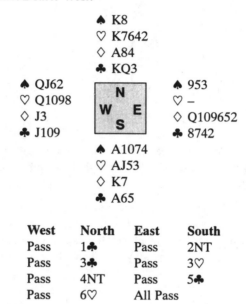

```
                    ♠ K8
                    ♡ K7642
                    ◇ A84
                    ♣ KQ3
    ♠ QJ62                         ♠ 953
    ♡ Q1098         N             ♡ –
    ◇ J3         W     E          ◇ Q109652
    ♣ J109          S             ♣ 8742
                    ♠ A1074
                    ♡ AJ53
                    ◇ K7
                    ♣ A65
```

West	North	East	South
Pass	1♣	Pass	2NT
Pass	3♣	Pass	3♡
Pass	4NT	Pass	5♣
Pass	6♡	All Pass	

Opening lead: ♣J

North upgraded his hand to open a strong club with the curious side effect that South got to bid hearts first.

Dummy's queen of clubs won the first trick and a small trump was led. The declarer intended to play South's jack if East played low. But East discarded a spade, and the declarer had to win with the ace of hearts.

The declarer reasoned that, to make the contract, West should hold exactly three clubs. West should also hold three spades and three diamonds, or four spades and two diamonds. In the latter case, the declarer should play the king and ace of spades, ruff a spade, cash the ace-king of clubs and ace-king of diamonds, and ruff the last spade.

Then, the situation became:

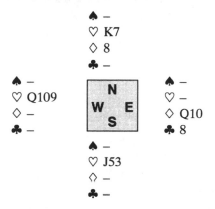

Dummy led the eight of diamonds, South ruffed with the three, and West would be thrown in the lead.

In the former case, i.e. if West held three spades and three diamonds, the declarer should cash spades, ruff a spade, cash clubs, cash diamonds, and ruff a diamond. Then, the situation became:

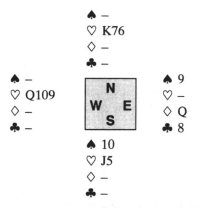

The ten of spades would now be led. If West ruffed with the nine, dummy should underruff, and North-South would win the last two tricks.

27
TWO WAY THROW-IN

Game All. Dealer East.

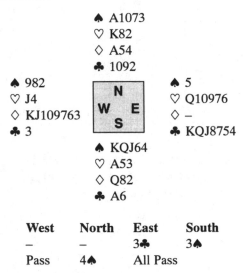

```
                    ♠ A1073
                    ♡ K82
                    ◊ A54
                    ♣ 1092
     ♠ 982              N              ♠ 5
     ♡ J4                              ♡ Q10976
     ◊ KJ109763     W     E            ◊ —
     ♣ 3               S              ♣ KQJ8754
                    ♠ KQJ64
                    ♡ A53
                    ◊ Q82
                    ♣ A6
```

West	North	East	South
–	–	3♣	3♠
Pass	4♠	All Pass	

Opening lead: ♣3

The declarer won the opening lead and cleared the trumps in three rounds, East discarding two clubs.

A diamond was led to dummy's ace, and East discarded another club.

The declarer knew at once that West held originally seven diamonds. He had shown three spades and a club, so he could not have more than two hearts. The declarer played the ace and king of hearts, West followed with the four and the jack, and the following ending was reached:

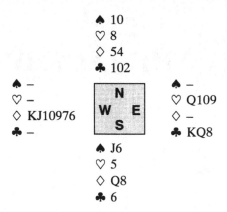

♠ 10
♡ 8
◇ 54
♣ 102

♠ –
♡ –
◇ KJ10976
♣ –

♠ –
♡ Q109
◇ –
♣ KQ8

♠ J6
♡ 5
◇ Q8
♣ 6

The declarer now led the five of hearts. East won and cashed the king of clubs. When East continued with the queen of clubs, South discarded a diamond. At the next trick East had to lead a heart or a club to give North-South a ruff and discard.

In the above position, the declarer could also lead a diamond to make the contract. West would win two diamond tricks and lead a third diamond to give North-South a ruff and discard.

28

LET THE JACK DIE

Game All. Dealer East.

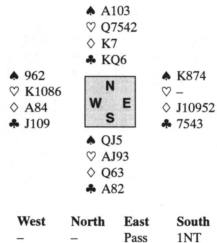

	♠ A103	
	♡ Q7542	
	◇ K7	
	♣ KQ6	

♠ 962		♠ K874
♡ K1086	N	♡ –
◇ A84	W E	◇ J10952
♣ J109	S	♣ 7543

	♠ QJ5	
	♡ AJ93	
	◇ Q63	
	♣ A82	

West	North	East	South
–	–	Pass	1NT
Pass	2◇	Pass	2♡
Pass	4♡	All Pass	

Opening lead: ♣J

North's two diamond bid was game-forcing Stayman showing at least five
hearts. The declarer won the first trick with the queen of clubs and led the
two of hearts, East discarding a diamond. South played the ace of hearts
and led the queen of spades to the two, three and king. East returned the
jack of diamonds, which dummy's king won. After the ace-jack of spades
and ace-king of clubs were cashed, the declarer led the seven of diamonds
from dummy, and West won South's queen with the ace. West returned a
diamond, which dummy ruffed. The position was:

```
              ♠ —
              ♡ Q75
              ◇ —
              ♣ —
  ♠ —                      ♠ 8
  ♡ K108      ┌─────┐      ♡ —
  ◇ —         │  N  │      ◇ J
  ♣ —         │W   E│      ♣ 7
              │  S  │
              └─────┘
              ♠ —
              ♡ J93
              ◇ —
              ♣ —
```

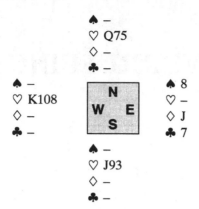

Now the declarer led a small heart from dummy and played the jack in the closed hand. It didn't matter whether West took the king of hearts or not, it was the only trick he was going to make.

29
OVERRUFFING

North-South Game. Dealer East.

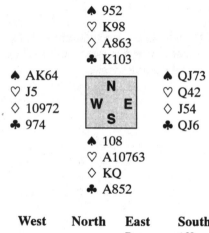

                    ♠ 952
                    ♡ K98
                    ◇ A863
                    ♣ K103

    ♠ AK64   ♠ QJ73
    ♡ J5   N   ♡ Q42
    ◇ 10972   W   E   ◇ J54
    ♣ 974   S   ♣ QJ6

                    ♠ 108
                    ♡ A10763
                    ◇ KQ
                    ♣ A852

West	North	East	South
–	–	Pass	1♡
1♠	2♡	2♠	3♡
Pass	4♡	All Pass	

Opening lead: ♠K

West led three rounds of spades, the declarer ruffed the third round. The king-queen of diamonds and ace-king of clubs were cashed. The declarer played the ace of diamonds at Trick 8, a club was discarded in the closed hand, and both opponents followed. The position was as follows:

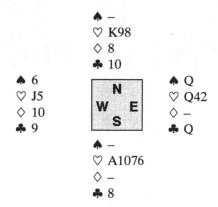

```
              ♠ —
              ♡ K98
              ◇ 8
              ♣ 10
♠ 6                        ♠ Q
♡ J5                       ♡ Q42
◇ 10                       ◇ —
♣ 9                        ♣ Q
              ♠ —
              ♡ A1076
              ◇ —
              ♣ 8
```

Dummy led the 10 of clubs, East's queen winning. If East led a trump, North-South could win all four trump tricks though declarer would have had to guess well if East led the trump queen. If East led the queen of spades, South would ruff low. Dummy should overruff this trick with the eight or nine of hearts and lead the diamond. Now if East ruffed low, South would overruff with a small trump and win the last two tricks with the ace-king of trumps. If East ruffed with the queen, South would overruff with the ace and take a finesse against West's jack at the next trick.

30
LET HIM BARE THE ACE

Game All. Dealer West.

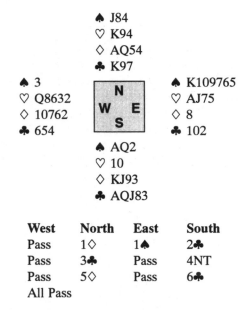

```
               ♠ J84
               ♡ K94
               ◇ AQ54
               ♣ K97
♠ 3                              ♠ K109765
♡ Q8632        N                ♡ AJ75
◇ 10762      W   E              ◇ 8
♣ 654          S                ♣ 102
               ♠ AQ2
               ♡ 10
               ◇ KJ93
               ♣ AQJ83
```

West	North	East	South
Pass	1◇	1♠	2♣
Pass	3♣	Pass	4NT
Pass	5◇	Pass	6♣
All Pass			

Opening lead: ♠3

The opening lead looked like a singleton. The declarer won East's nine of spades with the queen and cleared the trumps in three rounds. The declarer then conceded a heart trick and made the contract through a simple squeeze against East. Dummy's last three cards were the king of hearts, the jack of spades and the ace of diamonds. East had the ace of hearts and the king-ten of spades left. The declarer's cards were the ace-two of spades and the nine of diamonds. West's cards were immaterial. The ace of diamonds was played at Trick 11 and East was squeezed in spades and hearts.

South can make the contract in a different way. After drawing trumps he can cash four diamond tricks and play another trump winner to arrive at this position:

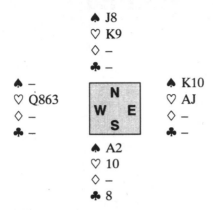

♠ J8
♥ K9
♦ –
♣ –

♠ –   ♠ K10
♥ Q863   ♥ AJ
♦ –   ♦ –
♣ –   ♣ –

♠ A2
♥ 10
♦ –
♣ 8

Now the eight of clubs is played, North discarding the nine of hearts, and East is squeezed. If East discards the jack of hearts, South will lead the ten of hearts to throw East in, and East will be obliged to lead away from his king-ten of spades. If East discards the ten of spades, South will win two spade tricks.

While this 'strip-squeeze and throw-in' may look elegant, there really is nothing to choose between the plays. Both succeed because East has the remaining spades and the ace of hearts. Indeed, in many ways the simple squeeze play is superior because, when South leads the ten of hearts, it would be a great play from West to duck smoothly if he held the ace.

31
SAFETY

East-West Game. Dealer North.

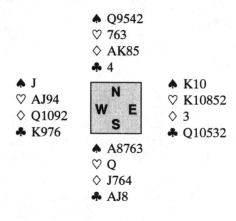

```
              ♠ Q9542
              ♡ 763
              ◇ AK85
              ♣ 4
  ♠ J                        ♠ K10
  ♡ AJ94          N          ♡ K10852
  ◇ Q1092     W     E        ◇ 3
  ♣ K976          S          ♣ Q10532
              ♠ A8763
              ♡ Q
              ◇ J764
              ♣ AJ8
```

West	North	East	South
–	Pass	Pass	1♠
Dble	Rdbl	3♡	Pass
Pass	4♠	All Pass	

Opening lead: ♡A

The first five tricks are:

> Trick 1, ace of hearts;
> Trick 2, heart continuation, ruffed;
> Trick 3, ace of spades;
> Trick 4, spade losing to the king;
> Trick 5, club switch taken by the ace.

How should South play?

The declarer should ruff two clubs and a heart and cash the ace of diamonds to reach this ending:

♠ Q
♡ –
◇ K85
♣ –

♠ 8
♡ –
◇ J76
♣ –

Now a small diamond is led from dummy. If East follows low, South plays the jack. If this loses then the diamonds must be breaking 3-2. If East shows out, South follows with a low diamond and West who must win will be endplayed. A diamond lead presents the declarer with a diamond trick; any other lead gives North-South a ruff and discard.

A good safety play and a pretty ending.

32
STRIP SQUEEZE

Game All. Dealer West.

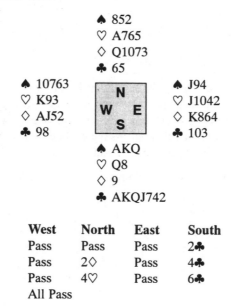

```
                    ♠ 852
                    ♡ A765
                    ◊ Q1073
                    ♣ 65
    ♠ 10763                        ♠ J94
    ♡ K93          N               ♡ J1042
    ◊ AJ52      W     E            ◊ K864
    ♣ 98           S               ♣ 103
                    ♠ AKQ
                    ♡ Q8
                    ◊ 9
                    ♣ AKQJ742
```

West	North	East	South
Pass	Pass	Pass	2♣
Pass	2◊	Pass	4♣
Pass	4♡	Pass	6♣
All Pass			

Opening lead: ♣9

After opening with a general game force, South's jump set clubs as trumps and commanded that North cuebid an ace if he had one. Already fortunate to survive this gambit, successfully South gilded the lily and went for the slam.

The declarer could make the contract if East had the ace-king of diamonds and king of hearts. In this case East could be forced to discard a top winner in diamonds and then thrown in to lead away from his king-small of hearts. But the chances were against it since East had not doubled North's five diamond bid. Of course, if West held the ace-king of diamonds and king of hearts, the same play would succeed, and West would be caught in a positional simple squeeze in hearts and diamonds. But the chances were also against it, because in that case West would certainly have chosen to lead a top diamond.

Was there any way to make the contract as the cards lay?

The declarer could play six rounds of trumps and cash the spade winners to arrive at the following ending:

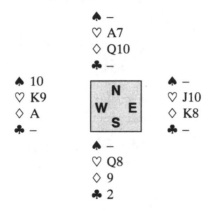

The two of clubs would be led and West would be squeezed. If he discards the nine of hearts, dummy's ace and South's queen of hearts would win two tricks. If he discards his spade winner, dummy would throw a diamond, and a diamond would be led to throw West in. If he discarded the ace of diamonds, dummy would throw the seven of hearts. The declarer then would lead the nine of diamonds to East's king, establishing a diamond trick, and dummy would win the last two tricks.

This is a strip squeeze because West is stripped of his exit cards, or a side suit winner in this case, and then thrown in to lead away from his guarded honour.

33

AN INVALUABLE LOSER

Love All. Dealer South.

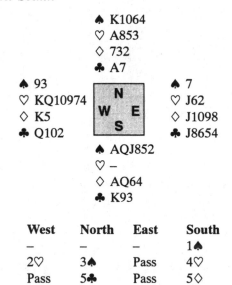

                    ♠ K1064
                    ♡ A853
                    ◇ 732
                    ♣ A7

    ♠ 93   ♠ 7
    ♡ KQ10974   ♡ J62
    ◇ K5   ◇ J1098
    ♣ Q102   ♣ J8654

                    ♠ AQJ852
                    ♡ –
                    ◇ AQ64
                    ♣ K93

West	North	East	South
–	–	–	1♠
2♡	3♠	Pass	4♡
Pass	5♣	Pass	5◇
Pass	5♡	Pass	6♠
All Pass			

Opening lead: ♡K

The declarer discarded a diamond on dummy's ace of hearts, ruffed a heart, led a trump to dummy's ten, ruffed another heart, led a trump to dummy's king and ruffed dummy's last heart. The declarer now knew that West held six hearts and two trumps. He had five cards in the other two suits. The declarer played three rounds of clubs, dummy ruffing the third round. As West followed suit three times, he could not hold more than two diamonds. The declarer was almost certain that West held the king of diamonds to justify his overcall, so the ace of diamonds was cashed and a small diamond led from the South hand. And that was how six hearts was made.

This hand occurred in a big event and was reported in some bridge columns. The declarer's reasoning and play were sound enough, but a better play would be to draw two rounds of trumps, ruff two hearts, and play three rounds of clubs, with dummy ruffing the third round. The position would be:

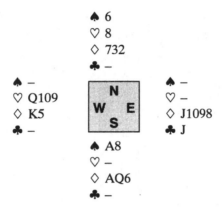

♠ 6
♡ 8
◇ 732
♣ –

♠ –
♡ Q109
◇ K5
♣ –

♠ –
♡ –
◇ J1098
♣ J

♠ A8
♡ –
◇ AQ6
♣ –

Now the eight of hearts would be led from dummy. When East failed to follow suit, the declarer would just discard the six of diamonds and claim the rest.

34
SURE-FIRE

Love All. Dealer South.

                    ♠ 8
                    ♡ A5
                    ◇ KQ8732
                    ♣ A1052

```
        N
     W     E
        S
```

                    ♠ A93
                    ♡ J6
                    ◇ AJ54
                    ♣ K763

West	North	East	South
–	–	–	1◇
Pass	5◇	All Pass	

Opening lead: ♠K

How should South play?

South should win the opening lead with the ace of spades and lead a spade, dummy ruffing with the queen of diamonds. The declarer draws trumps in two or three rounds, ending in the South hand. South's last spade is led and ruffed. After cashing the ace of hearts, the declarer must first play the ace or the king of clubs. Suppose East and West follow with the four and the eight of clubs. The declarer then leads a heart, allowing either of the opponents to win this trick. The position becomes:

♠ –
♡ –
◊ 8
♣ 1052

♠ –
♡ –
◊ 5
♣ K76

If West gets the lead and he leads a spade or a heart, North-South get a ruff and discard. If West leads the queen or the jack of clubs and East discards in spades or hearts, South ducks and can win all the rest. If West leads the nine of clubs, dummy covers with the ten. Whether the ten wins, or it is covered by the jack or queen and won with the king, the declarer has only one loser in clubs.

If East gets the lead, the result is the same: if East leads the queen or the jack of clubs, South must follow with a small club. Even if East leads from the queen-jack-nine of clubs, he can win only one club trick. If East leads the nine of clubs, South must also follow with a small club. In case the clubs are divided four and one, the ten will win this trick.

It must be noted that, before the throw-in play, it is absolutely necessary to cash one of the two top club winners. Otherwise, North-South may lose two tricks in clubs.

35
LONG SUIT WINNERS

Game All. Dealer North.

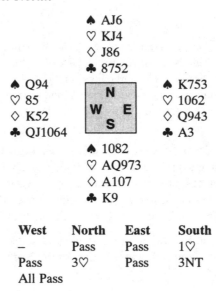

                    ♠ AJ6
                    ♡ KJ4
                    ◇ J86
                    ♣ 8752
    ♠ Q94   ♠ K753
    ♡ 85   N   ♡ 1062
    ◇ K52   W   E   ◇ Q943
    ♣ QJ1064   S   ♣ A3
                    ♠ 1082
                    ♡ AQ973
                    ◇ A107
                    ♣ K9

West	North	East	South
–	Pass	Pass	1♡
Pass	3♡	Pass	3NT
All Pass			

Opening lead: ♣Q

North's limit raise to three hearts on a flat hand with only three card support looks a bit unusual but North-South were playing five card majors, so it was only mildly eccentric.

East won the first trick with the ace of clubs and returned the three to South's king. Assuming the king and queen of spades are divided in the East-West hands, and the king and queen of diamonds are also divided in the East-West hands, how should South play? The declarer has eight top card winners. He can play five rounds of hearts. If West retains all his three club winners, he can only keep a total of three cards in spades and diamonds. Thus, he cannot guard both of the two suits. The declarer can create a ninth winner in the suit which West chooses to unguard. However, West must be kept out of the lead.

If West discards a club and retains two cards in both the spade and diamond suits, the situation is:

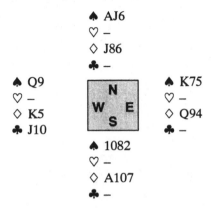

```
                    ♠ AJ6
                    ♡ –
                    ◊ J86
                    ♣ –
    ♠ Q9          ┌─────────┐    ♠ K75
    ♡ –           │    N    │    ♡ –
    ◊ K5          │ W     E │    ◊ Q94
    ♣ J10         │    S    │    ♣ –
                  └─────────┘
                    ♠ 1082
                    ♡ –
                    ◊ A107
                    ♣ –
```

Now the declarer can lead a small diamond from the closed hand. West can win this trick with the king of diamonds and cash two club winners, but North-South can win one spade and two diamond tricks. Alternatively, the declarer can lead a small spade from the closed hand at Trick 8. Dummy plays the jack if West plays low. East wins this trick with the king of spades, but North-South can win one diamond and two spade tricks later on.

36
LEADER'S TROUBLE

Love All. Dealer West.

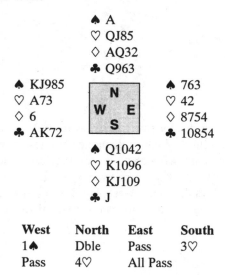

<pre>
              ♠ A
              ♡ QJ85
              ◇ AQ32
              ♣ Q963
  ♠ KJ985   ♠ 763
  ♡ A73   N   ♡ 42
  ◇ 6   W   E   ◇ 8754
  ♣ AK72   S   ♣ 10854
              ♠ Q1042
              ♡ K1096
              ◇ KJ109
              ♣ J
</pre>

West	North	East	South
1♠	Dble	Pass	3♡
Pass	4♡	All Pass	

Opening lead: ♣K

South was strong enough to bid three hearts. North naturally raised to four hearts.

West won the first trick with the king of clubs and switched to a small trump, which the declarer won. A trump was led, West won with the ace and led another trump. After the ace of spades and four diamond tricks were cashed, the situation became:

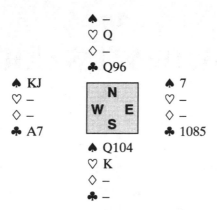

```
                    ♠ –
                    ♡ Q
                    ◇ –
                    ♣ Q96
    ♠ KJ                           ♠ 7
    ♡ –         ┌─────────┐        ♡ –
    ◇ –         │   N     │        ◇ –
    ♣ A7        │ W     E │        ♣ 1085
                │   S     │
                └─────────┘
                    ♠ Q104
                    ♡ K
                    ◇ –
                    ♣ –
```

Now the queen of spades was led, dummy discarding a club. West won this trick with the king of spades and was in trouble. If he led the jack of spades, dummy would ruff, and South's ten of spades would win a trick. If he led the ace of clubs, South would ruff, and dummy's queen of clubs would win a trick. And if he led the seven of clubs, dummy would put on the queen.

37
THE DEVIL'S COUP

Love All. Dealer East.

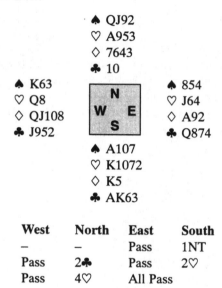

```
              ♠ QJ92
              ♡ A953
              ◇ 7643
              ♣ 10
  ♠ K63         N        ♠ 854
  ♡ Q8      W       E    ♡ J64
  ◇ QJ108              ◇ A92
  ♣ J952        S        ♣ Q874
              ♠ A107
              ♡ K1072
              ◇ K5
              ♣ AK63
```

West	North	East	South
–	–	Pass	1NT
Pass	2♣	Pass	2♡
Pass	4♡	All Pass	

Opening lead: ◇Q

After find the major suit fit with the aid of Stayman, North took a shot at game. East won the opening lead with the ace of diamonds and returned the suit, South's king winning.

The declarer played the ace of clubs and ruffed a club in dummy. Dummy led the queen of spades to the four, seven and king. At Trick 6, West returned a diamond, which was ruffed by South. South made the routine play of drawing two rounds of trumps and cashing side suit winners, followed by cross-ruffing. The opponents won one trick each in spades, hearts and diamonds.

It can be shown that the loss of a trump trick could be avoided and the declarer would have made eleven tricks. The play of the first six tricks would be the same as before. The next three tricks should be the ace-ten of spades and the king of clubs, dummy discarding the jack of spades. At Trick 10, South's last club would be led and ruffed in dummy. The three-card end position would be:

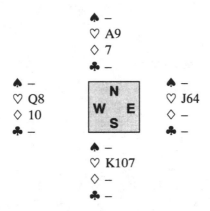

```
                    ♠ —
                    ♡ A9
                    ◇ 7
                    ♣ —
        ♠ —                         ♠ —
        ♡ Q8          N             ♡ J64
        ◇ 10      W       E         ◇ —
        ♣ —          S             ♣ —
                    ♠ —
                    ♡ K107
                    ◇ —
                    ♣ —
```

Dummy would lead the seven of diamonds. If East ruffed low, South would overruff and win the last two tricks with the ace-king of trumps. If East ruffed with the jack, South would overruff with the king, and a finesse could be taken against West's queen of hearts.

This is an attractive play to make an overtrick, an excellent way of garnering extra matchpoints in a pairs event but it is likely to prove to be a costly adventure playing teams or rubber bridge. For example, if West is able to ruff an early round of spades and declarer subsequently loses a trump trick, he will have put a laydown game on the floor.

38
NO SUITABLE DISCARD

North-South Game. Dealer West.

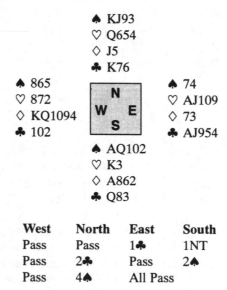

```
                    ♠ KJ93
                    ♡ Q654
                    ◇ J5
                    ♣ K76
    ♠ 865                         ♠ 74
    ♡ 872           N             ♡ AJ109
    ◇ KQ1094      W   E           ◇ 73
    ♣ 102           S             ♣ AJ954
                    ♠ AQ102
                    ♡ K3
                    ◇ A862
                    ♣ Q83
```

West	North	East	South
Pass	Pass	1♣	1NT
Pass	2♣	Pass	2♠
Pass	4♠	All Pass	

Opening lead: ◇K

The king of diamonds was allowed to hold the first trick. West continued with the queen of diamonds, the declarer won with the ace and ruffed a diamond with dummy's nine of spades, East discarding a club. A small heart was led from dummy, East played the ten, and South's king won. The declarer's last diamond was led and ruffed with dummy's jack of spades, and East discarded another club. Three rounds of trumps were then played, West followed three times, and East discarded a heart on the third round. The position was:

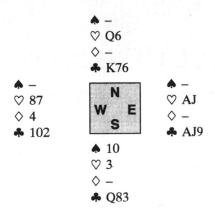

Now the ten of spades was played, dummy discarded a small club, and East could not find a suitable discard. If East discarded the jack of hearts, South could throw East in with the ace of hearts to lead away from his club holding. If East discarded the nine of clubs, South would lead a club, dummy playing the king. East could win this trick with the ace, or he could follow with the jack of clubs. In either case, his winning tricks would also be limited to just his two aces.

39
A COUPLE OF
VIENNA COUPS

North-South Game. Dealer East.

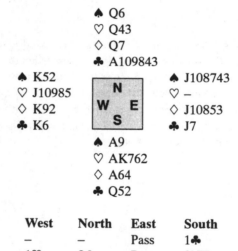

```
                    ♠ Q6
                    ♡ Q43
                    ◇ Q7
                    ♣ A109843
  ♠ K52                              ♠ J108743
  ♡ J10985          N               ♡ –
  ◇ K92          W     E            ◇ J10853
  ♣ K6              S               ♣ J7
                    ♠ A9
                    ♡ AK762
                    ◇ A64
                    ♣ Q52
```

West	North	East	South
–	–	Pass	1♣
1♡	2♣	Pass	2NT
Pass	3♣	Pass	3♡
Pass	3NT	Pass	4NT
Pass	5◇	Pass	6NT
All Pass			

Opening lead: ♡J

The declarer won the first trick with the king of hearts and led the two of clubs to the six, eight and jack. East returned a diamond, on which the declarer played the ace. The queen of clubs was led and West's king was taken by dummy's ace. The declarer now made the key play: he cashed the ace of spades. After that, the queen of hearts was cashed and the clubs were played off. West had to discard a heart on one of dummy's long clubs. The position at Trick 10 was:

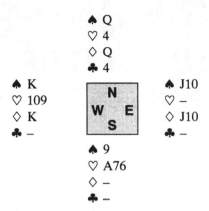

The last club winner was now led, South discarding the nine of spades, and West was squeezed in three suits. If West discarded a king, dummy would cash the queen of the discarded suit, and West would again be squeezed. If West discarded a heart, the declarer would win two extra heart tricks at once.

The contract was made through a rare play – a couple of Vienna Coups followed by a repeated squeeze.

40
THE GEM OF
A BRIDGE ENDING

Game All. Dealer West.

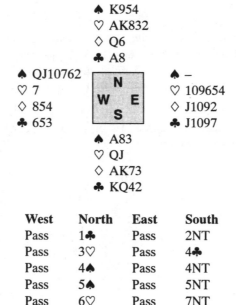

```
                    ♠ K954
                    ♡ AK832
                    ◇ Q6
                    ♣ A8
  ♠ QJ10762                        ♠ –
  ♡ 7             N                ♡ 109654
  ◇ 854        W     E             ◇ J1092
  ♣ 653           S                ♣ J1097
                    ♠ A83
                    ♡ QJ
                    ◇ AK73
                    ♣ KQ42
```

West	North	East	South
Pass	1♣	Pass	2NT
Pass	3♡	Pass	4♣
Pass	4♠	Pass	4NT
Pass	5♠	Pass	5NT
Pass	6♡	Pass	7NT
All Pass			

Opening lead: ♠Q

The declarer had twelve top card winners, two spades, four hearts, three diamonds and three clubs. East was void of spades, and on West's lead of the queen of spades he had to make a discard. In fact, East was squeezed in three suits at Trick 1. The declarer could gain an extra trick in whichever suit East might choose to discard.

Now suppose the opening lead is not a spade, perhaps North is the declarer at seven no trumps, then North-South can cash three winners in each of the heart, diamond and club suits to arrive at the following four-card ending:

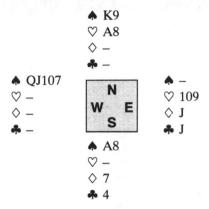

North:
♠ K9
♡ A8
♢ —
♣ —

West:
♠ QJ107
♡ —
♢ —
♣ —

East:
♠ —
♡ 109
♢ J
♣ J

South:
♠ A8
♡ —
♢ 7
♣ 4

The ace of spades or king of spades is played, and East is squeezed in three suits. If East discards a heart, North's eight of hearts wins an extra trick. If East discards the jack of diamonds or the jack of clubs, then South's seven of diamonds or four of clubs becomes a winner. This four-card triple squeeze ending is a real curiosity. There is no entry in any of the three single-menace suits. All the entries are provided in the fourth suit.

41
ANOTHER STRIP SQUEEZE

Love All. Dealer South.

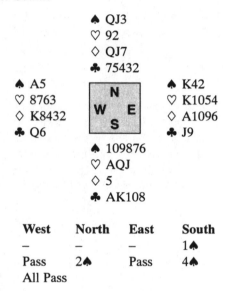

	♠ QJ3	
	♡ 92	
	◊ QJ7	
	♣ 75432	
♠ A5		♠ K42
♡ 8763		♡ K1054
◊ K8432		◊ A1096
♣ Q6		♣ J9
	♠ 109876	
	♡ AQJ	
	◊ 5	
	♣ AK108	

West	North	East	South
–	–	–	1♠
Pass	2♠	Pass	4♠
All Pass			

Opening lead: ♠A

The opponents played three rounds of trumps, and dummy won the third round. The declarer took a finesse in hearts, which worked. But the club suit was blocked so there was no further entry to dummy to repeat the finesse.

The declarer cashed all the club and spade winners, and the three-card end position was:

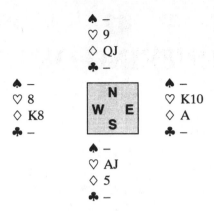

The five of diamonds was led, East's ace winning. He had to lead a heart into South's ace-jack.

If East made an early discard of the ace of diamonds to defend against the throw-in play, then the diamond lead at Trick 11 would be won by West's king. After that, if West led a diamond, dummy's queen would win a trick; if he led a heart, South's ace-jack would win two tricks.

Note that, if West's king and East's ace of diamonds were interchanged, the result would be the same. Note also that, if East blanks the king of hearts and West keeps two small hearts and the king of diamonds, then West will be endplayed with the king of diamonds.

42
RUFFING OUT

Love All. Dealer East.

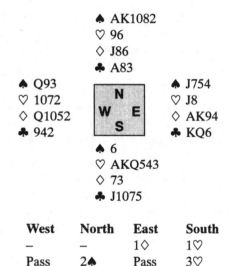

	♠ AK1082	
	♡ 96	
	◇ J86	
	♣ A83	
♠ Q93		♠ J754
♡ 1072		♡ J8
◇ Q1052		◇ AK94
♣ 942		♣ KQ6
	♠ 6	
	♡ AKQ543	
	◇ 73	
	♣ J1075	

West	North	East	South
–	–	1◇	1♡
Pass	2♠	Pass	3♡
Pass	4♡	All Pass	

Opening lead: ◇2

The opponents led three rounds of diamonds, South ruffing the third round. The declarer drew trumps in three rounds, dummy discarding a spade.

The declarer had nine tricks only. In order to set up a tenth winner, he had to play on the supposition that one of the opponents held four or more spades as well as the king-queen of clubs. The position was:

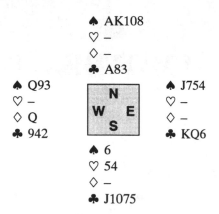

♠ AK108
♡ –
◊ –
♣ A83

♠ Q93   ♠ J754
♡ –   ♡ –
◊ Q   ◊ –
♣ 942   ♣ KQ6

♠ 6
♡ 54
◊ –
♣ J1075

North-South needed six tricks in this seven-card ending. The declarer now led the five of hearts throwing a club from dummy and East was squeezed in spades and clubs. If East discarded a spade, the declarer would cash the ace-king of spades, ruff a spade, setting up a spade winner in dummy. If East discarded a club, the declarer would cash the ace of clubs, concede a club trick to East and win the rest.

This is a form of the ruffing squeeze. It differs from an ordinary ruffing squeeze in that the declarer has a loser as the squeeze begins.

43
SMOTHER

East-West Game. Dealer North.

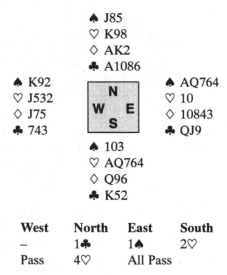

          ♠ J85
          ♡ K98
          ◇ AK2
          ♣ A1086

♠ K92   ♠ AQ764
♡ J532   ♡ 10
◇ J75   ◇ 10843
♣ 743   ♣ QJ9

          ♠ 103
          ♡ AQ764
          ◇ Q96
          ♣ K52

West	North	East	South
–	1♣	1♠	2♡
Pass	4♡	All Pass	

Opening lead: ♠2

East won the opening lead with the ace of spades and returned the six, which West's king won. West continued with the nine of spades, and East's queen was ruffed by the declarer. The declarer played the ace of hearts, which brought down West's two and East's ten.

The declarer had a club loser in the combined hands. He reasoned that the contract would only be in trouble if West had four hearts to the jack. However, in this case, the contract could probably be made by a throw-in play provided that East had the third round club winner.

Accordingly, he played the queen of hearts, on which East discarded a spade. The ace-king-queen of diamonds and ace-king of clubs were cashed, and both opponents followed suits. A third round of clubs was played at Trick 11, East won with the queen and he was on lead in this position:

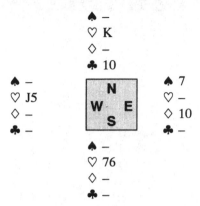

```
              ♠ —
              ♡ K
              ◇ —
              ♣ 10
   ♠ —                      ♠ 7
   ♡ J5      ┌─────────┐    ♡ —
   ◇ —       │  N      │    ◇ 10
   ♣ —       │ W    E  │    ♣ —
            │    S     │
             └─────────┘
              ♠ —
              ♡ 76
              ◇ —
              ♣ —
```

East led a spade or a diamond, South ruffed, and West had to overruff or underruff. In either case the declarer won the last two tricks.

44
SQUEEZE THROW-IN

Game All. Dealer West.

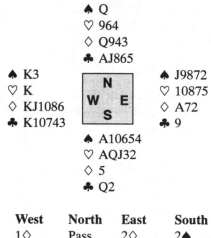

```
                    ♠ Q
                    ♡ 964
                    ◇ Q943
                    ♣ AJ865
    ♠ K3                          ♠ J9872
    ♡ K             N             ♡ 10875
    ◇ KJ1086     W     E          ◇ A72
    ♣ K10743        S             ♣ 9
                    ♠ A10654
                    ♡ AQJ32
                    ◇ 5
                    ♣ Q2
```

West	North	East	South
1◇	Pass	2◇	2♠
3♣	Dble	3◇	3♡
Pass	4♡	All Pass	

Opening lead: ◇J

Dummy covered the jack of diamonds with the queen, East won with the ace and returned a heart, on which South, taking into account the fact that West had opened the bidding, made the inspired shot of playing the two, West's king winning. West led the king of diamonds and South ruffed with the three of hearts. The queen of clubs was led, West covered with the king, and dummy's ace won, dropping East's nine. A spade was led to South's ace and a spade led and ruffed. The declarer then drew three rounds of trumps and on the third round the position was as follows:

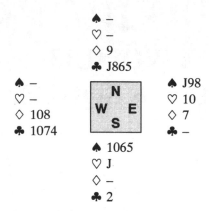

♠ –
♡ –
◇ 9
♣ J865

♠ –   ♠ J98
♡ –   ♡ 10
◇ 108   ◇ 7
♣ 1074   ♣ –

♠ 1065
♡ J
◇ –
♣ 2

On the lead of the last trump West was squeezed. If he discarded a club, dummy threw the diamond, and the declarer could take a finesse in clubs and win four club tricks. If West discarded a diamond, the declarer would lead the two of clubs, take a deep finesse in clubs, lead the nine of diamonds to throw West in, and win the last two tricks in dummy. The play is a combination of a squeeze and a throw-in.

45

TWO-SUIT DOUBLE SQUEEZE

Love All. Dealer West.

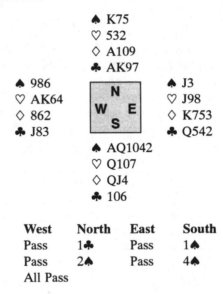

                    ♠ K75
                    ♡ 532
                    ◇ A109
                    ♣ AK97

    ♠ 986   ♠ J3
    ♡ AK64   ♡ J98
    ◇ 862   N   ◇ K753
    ♣ J83   W   E   ♣ Q542
                 S
                    ♠ AQ1042
                    ♡ Q107
                    ◇ QJ4
                    ♣ 106

West	North	East	South
Pass	1♣	Pass	1♠
Pass	2♠	Pass	4♠
All Pass			

Opening lead: ♠9

The declarer won the opening lead and took a finesse in diamonds. East won the king of diamonds and led the jack of hearts to South's queen and West's king. West returned a diamond. The declarer won with dummy's ace and drew two rounds of trumps.

Declarer eventually led a heart towards the ten and had to go one down. West had defended spectacularly well – first, he avoided leading either of his top heart honours and then when East switched to the jack of hearts he avoided continuing the suit. However, declarer could have actually made his contract in the following way.

If the ace of hearts was in the West hand and the nine-eight of hearts were in the East hand, both West and East would have to retain two cards in the heart suit. So it would be possible to form a double squeeze position against both opponents. The declarer should cash the last diamond winner and another trump to arrive at this situation:

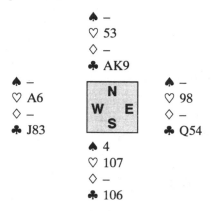

```
                    ♠ —
                    ♡ 53
                    ◇ —
                    ♣ AK9
        ♠ —                      ♠ —
        ♡ A6        N            ♡ 98
        ◇ —       W   E          ◇ —
        ♣ J83       S            ♣ Q54
                    ♠ 4
                    ♡ 107
                    ◇ —
                    ♣ 106
```

South would lead the four of spades and West would be squeezed. If he discarded the six of hearts, dummy would throw the nine of clubs and South would lead the seven of hearts to West's ace. The ten of hearts would become a winner. If West discarded a club, dummy would throw a heart, and East would be squeezed. Since he could not discard a club, he had to discard a heart. The declarer should then cash the ace-king of clubs before playing dummy's last heart and South would win the last trick with the seven of hearts to fulfil the four spade contract.

46
LONG LIVE THE KING

North-South Game. Dealer East.

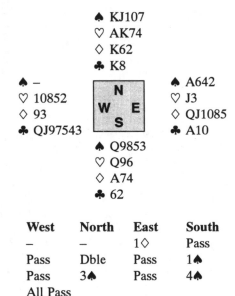

```
                    ♠ KJ107
                    ♡ AK74
                    ◊ K62
                    ♣ K8
    ♠ –                            ♠ A642
    ♡ 10852        N               ♡ J3
    ◊ 93         W   E             ◊ QJ1085
    ♣ QJ97543      S               ♣ A10
                    ♠ Q9853
                    ♡ Q96
                    ◊ A74
                    ♣ 62
```

West	North	East	South
–	–	1◊	Pass
Pass	Dble	Pass	1♠
Pass	3♠	Pass	4♠
All Pass			

Opening lead: ◊9

The first trick was won with the king of diamonds. Trumps were played, East's ace winning the third round. East led the queen of diamonds at Trick 5, declarer's ace winning. The declarer played another trump, followed by three rounds of hearts.

The contract would have been easy if the hearts had divided evenly. Unfortunately, East discarded a diamond on the third round of hearts. The position was:

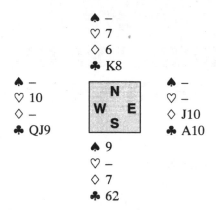

The seven of hearts was now played. The declarer could not be stopped from making two more tricks and the contract.

If East discarded a diamond, declarer should ruff. East would then be thrown in with a diamond and the dummy's king of clubs would make a trick. If East bared his ace of clubs, then the declarer, instead of ruffing, would discard the seven of diamonds. After West won this trick with the ten of hearts, he would have to lead a club, on which North would contribute the eight. East would have to win with the ace. The nine of spades and king of clubs would win the last two tricks.

47
PRESSURE ON BOTH OPPONENTS

East-West Game. Dealer North.

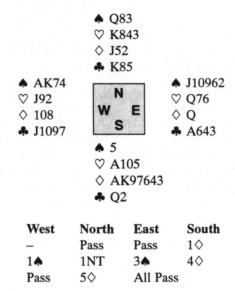

```
                    ♠ Q83
                    ♡ K843
                    ◇ J52
                    ♣ K85
   ♠ AK74                      ♠ J10962
   ♡ J92          N            ♡ Q76
   ◇ 108        W   E          ◇ Q
   ♣ J1097        S            ♣ A643
                    ♠ 5
                    ♡ A105
                    ◇ AK97643
                    ♣ Q2
```

West	North	East	South
–	Pass	Pass	1◇
1♠	1NT	3♠	4◇
Pass	5◇	All Pass	

Opening lead: ♠K

West won the first trick with the king of spades and switched to the jack of clubs, which the declarer's queen won. South played six rounds of diamonds reaching the following position:

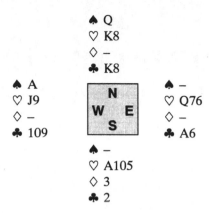

♠ Q
♡ K8
◇ –
♣ K8

♠ A   ♠ –
♡ J9   ♡ Q76
◇ –   ◇ –
♣ 109   ♣ A6

♠ –
♡ A105
◇ 3
♣ 2

In order to retain the ten and nine of clubs, West had discarded a heart. The declarer now played the three of diamonds, and West had to find a discard. Yet each discard was fatal to East-West. With the queen of spades in view in dummy, West could not afford to discard the ace of spades. If he discarded the nine of hearts, the declarer would lead the five of hearts to dummy's king and lead back the eight from dummy to take a finesse against East's queen. If he discarded a club, the declarer would lead the two of clubs to dummy's king and East's ace, establishing dummy's eight as a winner.

This is an unusual double guard squeeze situation with the guard squeeze against West. Unlike an ordinary double guard squeeze, here North-South have three winners out of the remaining five cards as the squeeze begins. A trick will be lost after the squeeze takes place.

48
TRUMP COUP OR DOUBLE SQUEEZE

East-West Game. Dealer East.

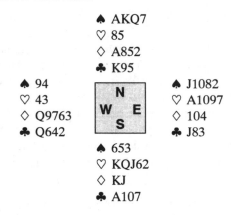

	♠ AKQ7	
	♡ 85	
	◇ A852	
	♣ K95	

♠ 94		♠ J1082
♡ 43		♡ A1097
◇ Q9763		◇ 104
♣ Q642		♣ J83

	♠ 653	
	♡ KQJ62	
	◇ KJ	
	♣ A107	

West	North	East	South
–	–	Pass	1♡
Pass	1♠	Pass	2♡
Pass	3◇	Pass	3NT
Pass	4NT	Pass	5◇
Pass	6♡	All Pass	

Opening lead: ♠9

Dummy won the first trick with the queen of spades and led a trump to South's jack. A spade was led to dummy's king and another trump led and won with South's queen. The declarer believed that East held the two missing trumps. He led a spade to dummy, ruffed the last spade, cashed the king and ace of diamonds, ruffed a diamond, cashed the ace and king of clubs, and, finally, ruffed another diamond. That was twelve tricks.

If East won his trump ace on the second trump lead, the declarer would no longer require the trump coup play. Suppose East led a diamond at Trick 5. The declarer should play the ace and king of diamonds, cash the ace of spades, and ruff a diamond to eliminate any diamond from the East hand. At this point, since East had no diamond left, he seemed to be squeezed in the black suits. But he could escape by playing a trump on the diamond lead. South would overruff and play another trump winner to arrive at this ending:

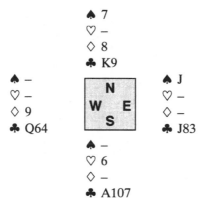

```
                    ♠ 7
                    ♡ —
                    ◇ 8
                    ♣ K9
    ♠ —                           ♠ J
    ♡ —          ┌─────────┐      ♡ —
    ◇ 9          │   N     │      ◇ —
    ♣ Q64        │ W   E   │      ♣ J83
                 │   S     │
                 └─────────┘
                    ♠ —
                    ♡ 6
                    ◇ —
                    ♣ A107
```

The opponents would be squeezed simultaneously on the lead of the six of hearts. West would have to hold on to the nine of diamonds otherwise dummy's eight would be good, so West would have to throw a club. Declarer would then be able to discard the diamond from the dummy and East would then be squeezed in spades and clubs.

49

THE PRECIOUS
EIGHT OF CLUBS

Love All. Dealer West.

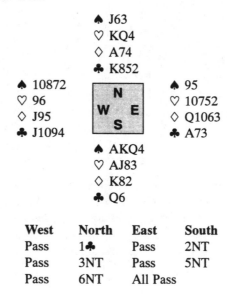

```
              ♠ J63
              ♡ KQ4
              ◇ A74
              ♣ K852
♠ 10872                      ♠ 95
♡ 96          N              ♡ 10752
◇ J95       W   E            ◇ Q1063
♣ J1094       S              ♣ A73
              ♠ AKQ4
              ♡ AJ83
              ◇ K82
              ♣ Q6
```

West	North	East	South
Pass	1♣	Pass	2NT
Pass	3NT	Pass	5NT
Pass	6NT	All Pass	

Opening lead: ♣J

The declarer won the first trick with the queen of clubs. He was quite certain that the ace of clubs was in the East hand, as it was most unlikely that West should lead the jack from ace-jack-ten against a six no trump contract, especially in dummy's bid suit.

The declarer hoped that West had the ten-nine of clubs, in this case the diamond and club suits were guarded by both opponents, and it was quite probable that neither of them could find an easy discard when the spade and heart winners were cashed.

The declarer cashed four spade winners and three heart winners, dummy discarding a club. The position was:

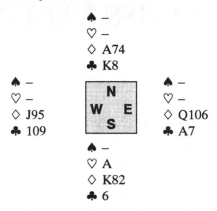

```
              ♠ —
              ♡ —
              ◊ A74
              ♣ K8
   ♠ —                      ♠ —
   ♡ —          N           ♡ —
   ◊ J95     W     E        ◊ Q106
   ♣ 109        S           ♣ A7
              ♠ —
              ♡ A
              ◊ K82
              ♣ 6
```

The ace of hearts was led, dummy discarded the worthless four of diamonds, and both opponents were squeezed simultaneously. If both West and East discarded in diamonds, the declarer could win three diamond tricks. If West discarded a club, the declarer could establish dummy's eight of clubs as a winner. If East discarded the seven of clubs, the declarer could lead the six of clubs to dummy's eight and East's ace, setting up the king.

50
CRISS-CROSS VARIATION

East-West Game. Dealer North.

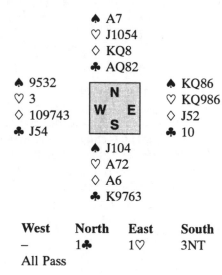

```
                    ♠ A7
                    ♡ J1054
                    ◇ KQ8
                    ♣ AQ82
       ♠ 9532                    ♠ KQ86
       ♡ 3          ┌─────┐      ♡ KQ986
       ◇ 109743     │  N  │      ◇ J52
       ♣ J54        │W   E│      ♣ 10
                    │  S  │
                    └─────┘
                    ♠ J104
                    ♡ A72
                    ◇ A6
                    ♣ K9763
```

West	North	East	South
–	1♣	1♡	3NT
All Pass			

Opening lead: ♡3

Two hearts would have been a more intelligent bid from South but he was fortunate to find such a good heart holding in the dummy.

The opening lead was covered by dummy's ten and East's queen, and the declarer ducked. East led the two of diamonds at Trick 2, and the declarer won with the ace. Three rounds of clubs were played, followed by two rounds of diamonds. The declarer cashed another club winner and the following ending was reached:

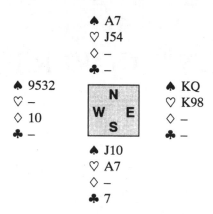

```
              ♠ A7
              ♡ J54
              ◊ −
              ♣ −
♠ 9532                      ♠ KQ
♡ −          ┌─────────┐   ♡ K98
◊ 10         │    N    │   ◊ −
♣ −          │ W     E │   ♣ −
             │    S    │
             └─────────┘
              ♠ J10
              ♡ A7
              ◊ −
              ♣ 7
```

On the lead of the seven of clubs, dummy discarded the seven of spades and East was squeezed. If he discarded a spade, the declarer could win two spade tricks. If he discarded a heart, the declarer could play the ace and then the seven of hearts to set up a heart winner in dummy. The declarer made a total of eleven tricks.

The above ending is a variation of the criss-cross squeeze. North-South have two losers as the squeeze begins. The squeeze gains a trick for the declarer.

Notice also that in this position, South could have also made the contract by playing two rounds of spades, forcing East to lead away from the king of hearts.

51
DON'T COVER IT

Game All. Dealer East.

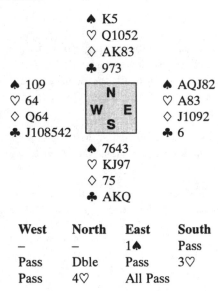

<pre>
                    ♠ K5
                    ♡ Q1052
                    ◊ AK83
                    ♣ 973
    ♠ 109   ♠ AQJ82
    ♡ 64   N   ♡ A83
    ◊ Q64   W   E   ◊ J1092
    ♣ J108542   S   ♣ 6
                    ♠ 7643
                    ♡ KJ97
                    ◊ 75
                    ♣ AKQ
</pre>

West	North	East	South
–	–	1♠	Pass
Pass	Dble	Pass	3♡
Pass	4♡	All Pass	

Opening lead: ♠10

Dummy played low at the first trick and East won with the jack. East played the ace and another trump. When the declarer led a spade to dummy's king and East's ace, East again led a trump. Since the declarer could not ruff two spades in dummy, he had only nine sure tricks. However, the declarer cashed the king of diamonds and the ace-king of clubs, leaving the following ending:

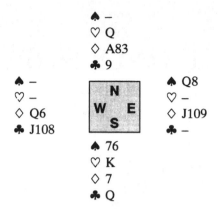

♠ –
♡ Q
◊ A83
♣ 9

♠ –   ♠ Q8
♡ –   ♡ –
◊ Q6   ◊ J109
♣ J108   ♣ –

♠ 76
♡ K
◊ 7
♣ Q

The declarer led the queen of clubs, then East was squeezed in spades and diamonds. If East discarded a spade, the declarer could ruff out a spade winner. If East discarded a diamond, the declarer could cash the ace of diamonds and ruff out a diamond winner.

This is a special form of the ruffing squeeze. Dummy has a three-card ruffing menace in diamonds, South has a two-card ruffing menace in spades. East is threatened in the two menace suits.

It is interesting to point out that, if dummy covered West's opening lead of the ten of spades with the king, the contract might be defeated. East could win with the ace and return his singleton club. After winning the trump lead, East could lead a small spade to West's nine to call for a club ruff.

52
THE ONLY HOPE

East-West Game. Dealer South.

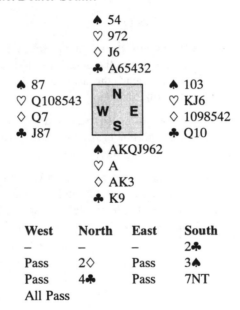

```
                      ♠ 54
                      ♡ 972
                      ◇ J6
                      ♣ A65432
        ♠ 87                        ♠ 103
        ♡ Q108543    N              ♡ KJ6
        ◇ Q7       W   E            ◇ 1098542
        ♣ J87        S              ♣ Q10
                      ♠ AKQJ962
                      ♡ A
                      ◇ AK3
                      ♣ K9
```

West	North	East	South
–	–	–	2♣
Pass	2◇	Pass	3♠
Pass	4♣	Pass	7NT
All Pass			

Opening lead: ♠8

In the light of North's initial two diamond negative, South's final bid was certainly of the optimistic variety; however, 'the play's the thing'.

The declarer won six spade tricks, cashed the two red aces, and the situation became:

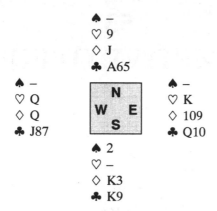

```
              ♠ —
              ♡ 9
              ◇ J
              ♣ A65
♠ —           ┌──────────┐         ♠ —
♡ Q           │    N     │         ♡ K
◇ Q           │ W     E  │         ◇ 109
♣ J87         │    S     │         ♣ Q10
              └──────────┘
              ♠ 2
              ♡ —
              ◇ K3
              ♣ K9
```

Analysis will show that this is a double clash squeeze position, which presents the only chance for making the contract. The diamond suit in the North-South hands is a clash menace against West, the nine of hearts is a one-card double menace, and the club suit is a split three-card menace against West.

On the lead of the two of spades West is clash-squeezed. If he discards the queen of diamonds, North's jack and South's king of diamonds can be made separately. If he discards a club, the declarer can win three club tricks. If he discards the queen of hearts, dummy must throw a club. Then, the king and ace of clubs are cashed, and on the lead of the ace of clubs East is squeezed in hearts and diamonds.

53
PRE-EMPTIVE OVERCALL

North-South Game. Dealer South.

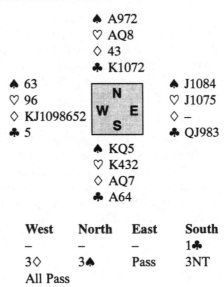

```
                    ♠ A972
                    ♡ AQ8
                    ◇ 43
                    ♣ K1072
      ♠ 63                        ♠ J1084
      ♡ 96            N           ♡ J1075
      ◇ KJ1098652  W   E          ◇ —
      ♣ 5             S           ♣ QJ983
                    ♠ KQ5
                    ♡ K432
                    ◇ AQ7
                    ♣ A64
```

West	North	East	South
–	–	–	1♣
3◇	3♠	Pass	3NT
All Pass			

Opening lead: ◇J

The declarer made the three no trump contract with an overtrick.

An analyst says that six no trumps can be made against any defence. How?

The declarer will know that West starts with eight diamonds because of East's discard at the first trick. The declarer should win Trick 1 with the queen of diamonds, and eliminate spades, hearts and clubs from the West hand. He cashes, in order, the king-queen of spades, the ace-queen of hearts, and the ace-king of clubs. West follows suit twice in spades, twice in hearts, and once in clubs. After that, the position becomes:

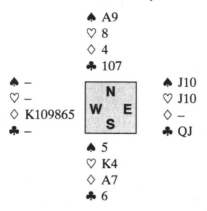

The four of diamonds is now led from dummy, East discards a club, South plays the seven of diamonds, and West's eight of diamonds wins. West is obliged to return a diamond to South's ace. At this trick – Trick 9 – dummy discards a club, and a repeated squeeze against East begins to operate.

If East discards a spade, the declarer will cash the ace and nine of spades, and on the nine of spades East will again be squeezed in hearts and clubs.

If East discards a heart, the declarer will cash the king and four of hearts, and on the four of hearts North discards the club and East will again be squeezed in spades and clubs.

Finally, if East discards the club, the declarer will cash the newly established club winner, and East will again be squeezed in spades and hearts.

Note that, if the opening lead is not a diamond, the declarer can make the six no trump contract in the same manner. The declarer may eliminate the spades, hearts and clubs in West's hand, lead a diamond from dummy, and play South's seven to throw West in. If West refuses to win, then the declarer will play the queen of diamonds at the next trick.

54
A HAND TO REMEMBER

Love All. Dealer South.

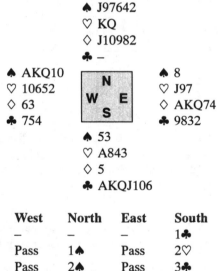

```
              ♠ J97642
              ♡ KQ
              ◊ J10982
              ♣ —
♠ AKQ10                      ♠ 8
♡ 10652        N             ♡ J97
◊ 63         W   E           ◊ AKQ74
♣ 754          S             ♣ 9832
              ♠ 53
              ♡ A843
              ◊ 5
              ♣ AKQJ106
```

West	North	East	South
–	–	–	1♣
Pass	1♠	Pass	2♡
Pass	2♠	Pass	3♣
Pass	3◊	Dble	3NT
All Pass			

Opening lead: ♠K

This hand was played by my friend, the late Mr Tze-kai Kiang, and was included in my book *The Squeeze at Bridge*. I repeat it here in memory of Mr Kiang.

West won the first trick with the king of spades and continued with the queen. East discarded the seven of diamonds. West led the six of diamonds to dummy's nine and East's queen. East could have won two more diamond tricks to set the three no trump contract, but he thought that no harm could be done by leading a heart to dummy's queen.

Tze-kai Kiang led dummy's jack of diamonds at Trick 5, and East won with the king and returned a club. The declarer won and played all his clubs. At Trick 11, he arrived at the following beautiful squeeze ending:

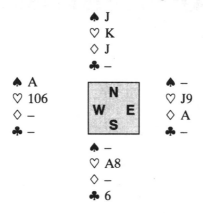

```
                    ♠ J
                    ♡ K
                    ◇ J
                    ♣ –
  ♠ A                              ♠ –
  ♡ 106         ┌─────────┐        ♡ J9
  ◇ –           │    N    │        ◇ A
  ♣ –           │ W     E │        ♣ –
                │    S    │
                └─────────┘
                    ♠ –
                    ♡ A8
                    ◇ –
                    ♣ 6
```

The six of clubs was led and West was squeezed. If West discarded the ace of spades, dummy's jack of spades would win a trick, with the king of hearts being the entry to dummy. If West discarded a heart, dummy would discard the jack of spades, and East would be squeezed. East could not discard the ace of diamonds, and a heart discard would enable the declarer to win the ace and eight of hearts in turn.

In those days we often called this ending a 'nosittej' double squeeze because it has the nature reverse to a jettison double squeeze. Maybe East will have learned an invaluable lesson: when you can see an easy way to beat a contract, take it.

55

HAPPY RETURN

East-West Game. Dealer North.

```
                    ♠ 10754
                    ♡ 983
                    ◇ 632
                    ♣ AKQ
              ┌───────────┐
              │     N     │
              │  W     E  │
              │     S     │
              └───────────┘
                    ♠ AKQ
                    ♡ AQ10
                    ◇ AJ7
                    ♣ 9653
```

West	North	East	South
–	Pass	Pass	2NT
Pass	3♣	Pass	3◇
Pass	3NT	All Pass	

Opening lead: ◇K

West's king of diamonds was allowed to win the first trick, and East followed with the five of diamonds. At Trick 2, West led a club, which dummy's queen won. The declarer played the ace-king of spades, and on the king of spades, West discarded the two of hearts. A club was led to dummy's king, and West discarded a diamond. The declarer led a heart from dummy, and South put on the ten, West's jack winning. West returned a heart, East followed with a small heart, and South's queen won.

The opponents' cards were now quite clear. East held originally five spades and five clubs, and he had followed to hearts twice. Therefore, the five of diamonds which he played at Trick 1 was a singleton.

The declarer now led the jack of diamonds to West's queen, and the position was:

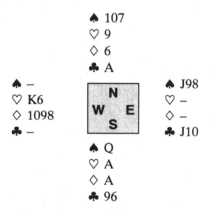

```
              ♠ 107
              ♡ 9
              ◇ 6
              ♣ A
   ♠ -                        ♠ J98
   ♡ K6        ┌─────┐        ♡ -
   ◇ 1098      │  N  │        ◇ -
   ♣ -         │W   E│        ♣ J10
              │  S  │
              └─────┘
              ♠ Q
              ♡ A
              ◇ A
              ♣ 96
```

West led a diamond or a heart to South's ace, East discarding a spade. At the next trick, the declarer led the other ace in the South hand, and East was squeezed in spades and clubs. If East discarded a spade, the declarer would play the queen of spades, and lead a club to dummy's ace to cash a spade winner. If East discarded a club, the declarer would first play the ace of clubs, and then lead a spade to South's queen to cash a club winner.

The play of this hand is a combination of a throw-in against West and a criss-cross squeeze against East. The throw-in occurred at Trick 6, and the squeeze took place at Trick 10.

56
GOD SAVE THE KING

East-West Game. Dealer South.

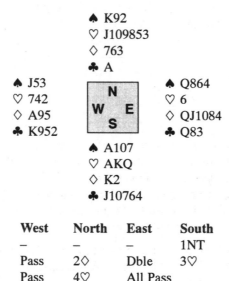

```
                    ♠ K92
                    ♡ J109853
                    ◇ 763
                    ♣ A
    ♠ J53            N           ♠ Q864
    ♡ 742        W      E        ♡ 6
    ◇ A95           S           ◇ QJ1084
    ♣ K952                       ♣ Q83
                    ♠ A107
                    ♡ AKQ
                    ◇ K2
                    ♣ J10764
```

West	North	East	South
–	–	–	1NT
Pass	2◇	Dble	3♡
Pass	4♡	All Pass	

Opening lead: ♡2

This hand appeared in *China Daily* some ten years ago. North's two diamonds was a transfer bid.

South won the opening lead and led a club to dummy's ace. Dummy led the three of diamonds, and the king was taken by West's ace. West led another heart. A club was ruffed in dummy and another diamond led. Now East followed with a low diamond, hoping that the nine of diamonds was not in the declarer's hand. West won with the nine of diamonds and led his third heart. So the contract was one down.

This hand was regarded as a gem of defensive play and the author said that there was no way for the declarer to avoid losing four tricks.

In fact, four hearts is a makeable contract. The correct play is as follows: Trick 1, the queen of hearts; Trick 2, the ace of clubs; Trick 3, the king of hearts; Trick 4, club ruff; Trick 5, the ace of hearts; Trick 6, club ruff. The remaining seven-card situation is:

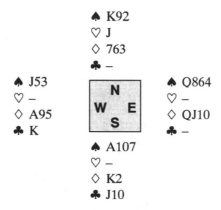

The two of spades is led from dummy. East has to play low, South plays the ten, and West wins with the jack. West's best return is a spade, and the declarer wins the two top spades. Up to this point, North-South have collected eight tricks. South then leads a club, which puts West in lead, dummy discarding a diamond. West can win one trick more with his ace of diamonds. South's king of diamonds and dummy's jack of hearts win the last two tricks. This makes the four heart contract.

The line of play adopted here is an avoidance play, i.e. to keep East out of the lead. Even if the declarer discovered that the king of clubs were in the East hand when he led a club from South at Trick 10, he could ruff it in dummy, and then he could still play for the last chance of the ace of diamonds lying in front of the king of diamonds. In that case, the king of diamonds would win the tenth trick to make the contract.

Notice also that, if West tries to get off play with the king of clubs at an earlier stage, declarer can ruff in dummy and still get to his hand with the ace of spades to cash the master club.

57

TRUMP OVERTAKING SQUEEZE

Game All. Dealer West.

```
                    ♠ 972
                    ♡ 7653
                    ◇ K654
                    ♣ A5
    ♠ 83             ┌─────────┐      ♠ J10654
    ♡ J1094          │    N    │      ♡ Q82
    ◇ 97             │ W     E │      ◇ 1032
    ♣ J10973         │    S    │      ♣ KQ
                     └─────────┘
                    ♠ AKQ
                    ♡ AK
                    ◇ AQJ8
                    ♣ 8642
```

West	North	East	South
Pass	Pass	Pass	2♣
Pass	2NT	Pass	3◇
Pass	4◇	Pass	4NT
Pass	5♡	Pass	6◇
All Pass			

Opening lead: ♣J

After diamonds were agreed, 4NT was Roman Keycard Blackwood and the response showed two out of five aces (the trump king counts as an ace) and denied the queen of trumps.

Dummy played low on West's jack of clubs. East won with the king and returned the queen to dummy's ace. The declarer played the ace and queen of trumps. Both opponents followed. The declarer had still two small clubs in his hand. If the last trump were in the West hand, the declarer could ruff two clubs with dummy's two trumps. But if East had the last trump, then it would be very dangerous to ruff the first club with dummy's small trump. Accordingly the declarer cashed the ace-king of hearts and ace-king-queen of spades. On the third round of spades West discarded a club, which proved that the cross-ruff plan could not succeed. The four-card end position was:

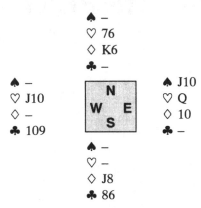

```
                 ♠ —
                 ♡ 76
                 ◇ K6
                 ♣ —
     ♠ —          N          ♠ J10
     ♡ J10                   ♡ Q
     ◇ —       W     E       ◇ 10
     ♣ 109        S          ♣ —
                 ♠ —
                 ♡ —
                 ◇ J8
                 ♣ 86
```

The jack of diamonds was now played, drawing East's last trump. West had to guard both the heart and the club suits, but he had to choose between discarding a heart and a club. If West discarded a club, North would follow with the six of diamonds, so that the lead would still be with South. South would lead a club and ruff it in dummy, setting up a club winner in the South hand. If West discarded a heart, dummy could overtake South's jack of diamonds with the king. Then, the declarer would lead a heart from dummy and ruff it in the South hand, setting up a heart winner in dummy.

This play can be called a trump overtaking ruffing squeeze.

58
AN IMPROVEMENT
IN THE PLAY

Love All. Dealer South.

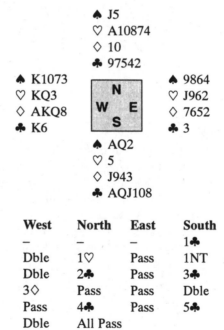

```
                    ♠ J5
                    ♡ A10874
                    ◇ 10
                    ♣ 97542
   ♠ K1073                          ♠ 9864
   ♡ KQ3           N                ♡ J962
   ◇ AKQ8        W   E              ◇ 7652
   ♣ K6            S                ♣ 3
                    ♠ AQ2
                    ♡ 5
                    ◇ J943
                    ♣ AQJ108
```

West	North	East	South
–	–	–	1♣
Dble	1♡	Pass	1NT
Dble	2♣	Pass	3♣
3◇	Pass	Pass	Dble
Pass	4♣	Pass	5♣
Dble	All Pass		

Opening lead: ◇K

I found this hand in a bridge publication. It was used to illustrate a kind of elimination play.

The king of diamonds held the first trick and West switched to the king of hearts which dummy's ace won. A heart was led and ruffed. The jack of diamonds was led and covered and ruffed in dummy. Another heart was ruffed, and the ace and queen of clubs were played. West won South's queen of clubs with the king. The situation was:

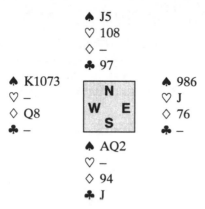

Now, if West led a spade, the declarer could win two spade tricks, ruff a spade, ruff a heart, and make good dummy's last heart. If West led the queen of diamonds, the declarer could ruff it in dummy, ruff out a heart winner, and discard a spade from dummy on the nine of diamonds. If West led the eight of diamonds, the declarer could let it run to his nine, discarding a spade from dummy, and ruff out a heart winner as before.

This was indeed a very good play. But a careful study will show that a more reasonable order of play is probably as follows: king of diamonds; ace of hearts; ace of clubs; diamond ruff; heart ruff; diamond ruff; heart ruff; diamond ruff. The position at Trick 9 is:

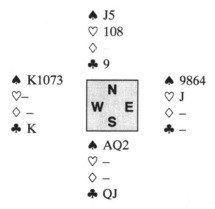

Dummy leads the eight of hearts for South to ruff. If West discards a spade, he will be thrown in with a club. The jack of spades and ten of hearts in dummy can always win two tricks. If, at Trick 9, West overruffs the heart lead, the result will be the same.

The advantage of this play is:

Firstly, West may hold four hearts instead of three. In this case, this play also works. In fact, the five club contract is ensured as soon as the declarer finds that both West and East follow suit when South's fourth diamond is led and ruffed. Of course, it is assumed that both black kings are in the West hand.

Secondly, if the queen of diamonds is in the East hand instead of being in the West hand, the result is the same.

If the West cards are 2-4-5-2, both plays fail. But if West's hand pattern is 3-4-4-2, the first play fails, while the second play succeeds.

59

ALL ROADS
LEAD TO ROME

Game All. Dealer East.

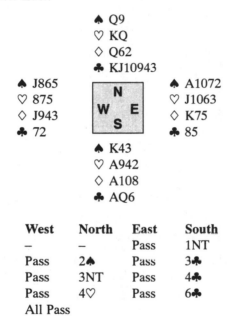

```
              ♠ Q9
              ♡ KQ
              ◇ Q62
              ♣ KJ10943
  ♠ J865                    ♠ A1072
  ♡ 875        N            ♡ J1063
  ◇ J943    W     E         ◇ K75
  ♣ 72         S            ♣ 85
              ♠ K43
              ♡ A942
              ◇ A108
              ♣ AQ6
```

West	North	East	South
–	–	Pass	1NT
Pass	2♠	Pass	3♣
Pass	3NT	Pass	4♣
Pass	4♡	Pass	6♣
All Pass			

Opening lead: ♡8

After South's strong no trump opening, North transferred to show clubs. South bid clubs to show some suitability but felt that he was worth another go when North bid 3NT. After all, what was the point of North showing his club suit at all if he wasn't interested in higher things.

The declarer won the first trick with dummy's queen of hearts, cashed the king of hearts, and led the nine of spades. If East held the ace of spades and played it at once, the contract would be easy, as dummy's two diamonds could be discarded under South's king of spades and ace of hearts. However, the declarer's king of spades won Trick 3, which proved that the ace of spades was really in the East hand.

In order to make the contract, the declarer hoped that East held, in addition to the ace of spades, the king of diamonds. In this case, the declarer could play the hand in different ways.

The first line of play was to cash the ace of hearts (dummy discarding the queen of spades at this trick), ruff a spade, lead a club to South's queen, ruff another spade, and lead a club to South's ace. The position would be:

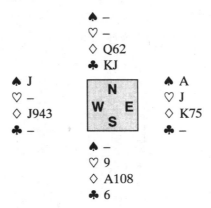

Now the declarer could lead the nine of hearts and discard a diamond in dummy to throw East in. East would either lead a diamond from the king or give the declarer a ruff and discard.

The second line of play was to discard dummy's two of diamonds under South's ace of hearts, and play on clubs to arrive at this ending:

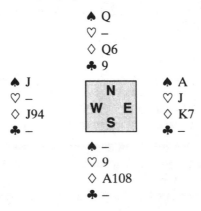

Now the declarer could lead the nine of clubs, and East would be subjected to a triple squeeze. A heart or diamond discard would give the declarer an extra trick. And a spade discard would be even worse: dummy's queen of spades would squeeze East a second time.

The declarer could also play the hand in the following way. After cashing the king-queen of hearts, he could play a club to South's queen, lead a spade to dummy's queen and East's ace, win East's return, clear the outside trumps, cash the ace of hearts or/and king of spades, and play on trumps. Dummy's last three cards would be the queen-six of diamonds and a trump. South's cards would be the ace-ten of diamonds and the nine of hearts. And East's cards would be the king-seven of diamonds and the jack of hearts. East would be caught in a positional simple squeeze in diamonds and hearts.

60
THE PERKINS COUP

Love All. Dealer East.

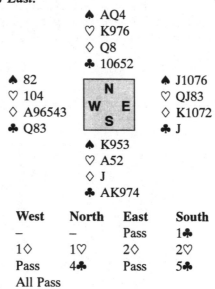

	♠ AQ4	
	♡ K976	
	◊ Q8	
	♣ 10652	
♠ 82		♠ J1076
♡ 104		♡ QJ83
◊ A96543		◊ K1072
♣ Q83		♣ J
	♠ K953	
	♡ A52	
	◊ J	
	♣ AK974	

West	North	East	South
–	–	Pass	1♣
1◊	1♡	2◊	2♡
Pass	4♣	Pass	5♣
All Pass			

Opening lead: ◊A

West won the first trick and continued with the five of diamonds to dummy's queen and East's king, which the declarer ruffed. The declarer played the ace and king of trumps, East discarding a diamond on the second round. There was a loser in trumps.

Since West had overcalled two diamonds, he probably had five or six cards in diamonds. Since he had also three clubs, his major suits should be relatively short. The declarer planned to eliminate the spades and hearts from the West hand. Accordingly, the king-queen of spades and ace-king of hearts were cashed. After that, a club was led, and West's queen won. The position was:

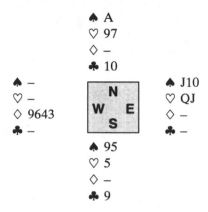

West had nothing but diamonds to lead. Dummy ruffed the diamond lead with the ten of clubs, South discarded the five of hearts, and East was squeezed in spades and hearts. If East discarded a spade, the declarer could cash dummy's ace of spades and cross to the closed hand to make a spade trick. If East discarded a heart, the declarer could lead and ruff a heart and make good dummy's last heart.

This play is called the Perkins Coup. It was first discovered by Frank K. Perkins. In reality, this play is a variation of a ruffing squeeze. A typical ruffing squeeze situation can be seen simply by changing North's ten of clubs to the ten of diamonds and South's five of hearts to the two of diamonds, while the lead can be with South or North or West:

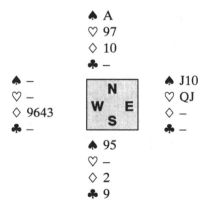

The clubs are trumps. A diamond is led to North's ten and East is ruffing-squeezed. This is one of the simplest basic forms of the ruffing squeeze.